Praise for *A Lesbian Belle Tells*

"Elizabeth's passionate advocacy for storytelling is nothing less than spot on. Her words chronicle her personal healing over a lifetime. There is healing in the telling and the being heard. In her memoir, which so beautifully comes full circle, Elizabeth's entertaining way of brewing poignancy and hope from difficult and lighthearted stories replete with Southern eccentricities offers each of us some hard-earned, life-giving messages. What this lesbian belle tells are universal truths that resonate with all of us. The Deep South part may be more colorful for those of us who know it first-hand, but the shared human parts of love and belonging shine brightly as she invites us all to weave our own stories toward wholeness."

Karole Sessums,
Author of *Backyards and Beyond: Mississippians and Their Stories*

"Elizabeth McCain has written a memoir of moments, tracing her journey from naive and intelligent Southern belle to a passionately spiritual and witty lesbian, still connected to her Southern roots. She is a sophisticated storyteller with a knack for capturing the transgressive and touching encounters of coming out, falling in love, and claiming her place in the world. Sharing and celebrating the power of story is her calling, and we are all the better for that!"

Carol Burbank, Ph.D.
Storyweaving Coach,
Author of *Storyweaving Playbook One: Answer the Call to Adventure*

"Elizabeth is a gifted storyteller. In these pages, she pours out hers – the hurt, the heartache, and the triumph. We feel with her, not only because she puts her heart into her words, but because her story is ours as well. The longing to be seen and known. Accepted and loved. So, find a porch. And a rocking chair. And a glass of sweet tea. Because Elizabeth's tales are worth savoring."

Ginger M. Sullivan,
Psychotherapist and Author of *The Road Out: Musings of a Southern Wanderlust*

"I laughed, I cried. I was mesmerized. Elizabeth is a tremendously gifted wordsmith. Her stories are open, honest, and will tug at your heartstrings, evoking imagery of what it was like growing up and evolving within the rigid constraints of Southern culture amid the pride, prejudice, and burden of the status quo. Her indomitable spirit and sense of humor shine through and perfectly balance the poignancy of coming out in the Deep South, when men wore the pants, and woman's place was in the kitchen. Each story is a delicious morsel to relish and enjoy."

Jamie Fox,
DJ, Entertainer

"You don't have to be from the South, or a lesbian, to be immediately drawn into *A Lesbian Belle Tells*. The eccentricities, humor, and warmth of characters in Elizabeth's life, as well as her journey of becoming her truest, best self, won't let you go. Bittersweet, funny, and hopeful, it is a *Steel Magnolias* for the new decade."

Tim Gilham, Artistic Director
New Wave Singers of Baltimore
John Knapp, Former Artistic Director
Richmond Triangle Players

"Elizabeth is a natural storyteller. In this memoir, she possesses a magical power to immediately grab your attention, invite you into her world, and make you never want to leave. She's a keen observer of human behavior, which shows in how she brings vivid and distinct characters to life. Her voice is authentic and charming, as she shares an honest, touching, and thought-provoking perspective on life as a 'lesbian belle' in the American South, and in Washington, DC."

Amy Saidman,
Artistic Executive Director, Story District

"Elizabeth is an amazing storyteller. As I read *A Lesbian Belle Tells*, I felt that I was sitting on a comfy sofa, having tea with a dear friend. Written with raw, heart-centered authenticity, Elizabeth shares stories from her past that have influenced and inspired her to become the woman she is today. No matter what your sexual orientation, this memoir will keep you deeply engaged. It is a reminder that as human beings, we have more in common than we often acknowledge."

Deb Barnett, Ph.D.
Psychologist

"I love Elizabeth's stories! Reading this book is like sitting on a porch having the pleasure of listening to a talented storyteller weave her magic of memory. Elizabeth makes the personal universal through powerful language that accesses not only the shape of her tales but also the many emotional threads that bind them together. This memoir sparked my own memories of coming out in a religious household in the early 80s. I just wish I'd had Elizabeth's humorous lens! I encourage you to read this delightfully wise and entertaining book."

Barbara Bingham,
Imago Educator

"Elizabeth McCain's memoir, *A Lesbian Belle Tells*, shows the vital importance that everyone, no matter who they are, needs to tell their stories. Elizabeth combines humor, deep sadness, gifted insight, and humility to remind us all of the power of story. For me personally, this book helped me tell my own story in a new and more open way. It helped me look at the moments of pain, loss and rejection as the vital ingredients to creating the woman I am today. Do yourself a favor. Read this book and then sit down and write your own story. Find in your own story the ability to forgive yourself and others, to see all the aspects of your story, both joyful and painful and in between as vital elements to creating the unique 'you'. While Elizabeth's memoir is about coming out as a lesbian, it is so much more. It is about how our common humanity unites us and how much we all want to belong and be loved. It includes the life lessons we can all learn. And if we listen, we can truly find a place inside us of deep belonging and connection to all things."

Maya Kollman,
Imago Therapist and Master Trainer

"Elizabeth McCain's memoir takes the reader on the uncertain path of coming to loving terms with one's sexuality, as well as coming out to her family and the world. Her path is one of acceptance, courage, faith, forgiveness, and love. Within each chapter lie characters and situations that entertain and challenge us. She skillfully captures the positive and the negative in a balanced way. One is reminded that the way to connection is through sincere and often difficult dialogue, forgiveness and letting go, and wanting to love more than wanting to be right. A good reminder for the divisive times in which we find ourselves. Elizabeth's journey is courageous, and can serve as a guide to the LGBTQ+ folks. It serves as a reminder to everyone that love is greater than fear."

> Beth Ohlsson,
> Speaker, Storyteller, Counselor, and
> Author of *Distilling Hope: 12 Stories to
> Distill the 12 Steps*

"Regardless of who you love, you'll love these stories. Elizabeth McCain's hilariously heartbreakingly true stories will not only entertain you, but they will also enlighten you, heal you, and if you're extra lucky, inspire you to share your own stories, bless your heart."

> Stephanie Garibaldi,
> Storytelling Teacher, Trainer, and
> Director

"Following in the venerable footsteps of other strong Southern women writers like Julia Reed, Elizabeth McCain tells stories about the South as only Southern women can – with humor and poignancy. But Elizabeth McCain isn't Julia Reed – she's a fabulous lipstick lesbian! She's also an uninhibited writer who opens her life story to readers: the often hilarious, sometimes difficult, occasionally raw, but always heartfelt truth of her life. *A Lesbian Belle Tells* is the story of the overwhelming redemption of love, of learning to love whom one wants to love, and of learning to love oneself."

Bette L. Bottoms, Ph.D.
Editor of *The Legacy of Racism for Children:*
Psychology, Law, and Public Policy
Professor of Psychology, University
of Illinois at Chicago

"Elizabeth McCain is a powerful storyteller who brings tears, laughter, and deep introspective insights into her writing. In her memoir, she accesses grief the way a miner goes after diamonds: unafraid to give the unvarnished truth of her life, loves, and losses. Each story resonates within my soul and speaks to my own trials in this Earthly realm. Elizabeth made me laugh so hard, while at the same time, expanded my heart and made me understand how hard it is to come out in a less than hospitable environment. She continues to change lives and gives hope to those who may otherwise give up. Elizabeth is my heroine."

Ruth Souther,
Author of *Vega's Path: The Elemental*
Priestess and *The Heart of Tarot*

"You will laugh, cry, and be mesmerized by these stories."
— Jamie Fox, Entertainer

A Lesbian Belle Tells

OUTrageous Southern Stories of Family, Loss, and Love

Elizabeth McCain

A Lesbian Belle Tells

OUTrageous Southern Stories
of Family, Loss, and Love

Published by
Crystal Heart Imprints
Springfield, IL

A Lesbian Belle Tells
OUTrageous Southern Stories of Family, Loss, and Love

ISBN: 978-1-945567-23-0
Library of Congress Control Number: 2020903749

Printed in the United States of America, 2020

Cover Design: Heidi Fosnaught
Cover Photo: Steven Parke

This Book Is Lovingly Dedicated To:

Marie, my soulmate and anchor, who has given me a new story to live;

Anne Thomas, a gifted storyteller and dear friend, who encouraged me;

My Southern ancestors, my parents, Marguerite Cooper McCain and James Everett McCain, Jr. (Mama and Daddy), as well as Aunt Liber, and Aunt Frannie, whose passion for porch stories told at "Southern Comfort" inspired, entertained, and comforted me;

And to LGBTQ+ people for your courage, strength, and commitment to loving fiercely.

TABLE OF CONTENTS

"*Owning our story can be hard, but not nearly as difficult as spending our lives running from it. Embracing our vulnerabilities is risky but not nearly as dangerous as giving up on love and belonging and joy – the experiences that make us the most vulnerable. Only when we are brave enough to explore the darkness, will we discover the power of our light.*"

— **Brené Brown,**
Daring Greatly: How the Courage to Be Vulnerable Transforms the Way We Live, Love, Parent, and Lead

"*I hope you will go out and let stories happen to you, and that you will work them, water them with your blood and tears and your laughter till they bloom, till you yourself burst into bloom.*"

— **Clarissa Pinkola Estés, Ph.D.**
Women Who Run With the Wolves: Myths and Stories of the Wild Woman Archetype

"*Stories will chase you, follow you, appear to you and ask you to be told, shared, written down…Let all these stories inspire you to spend your time more richly, and let that richness spill onto your pages. Let your stories of change and stumbling illuminate the path for those looking behind you. Writing lights a bright beam for all to see, and that light leads more souls sharing their experiences.*"

— **SARK,**
Juicy Pens, Thirsty Paper: Gifting the World with Your Words and Stories, and Creating the Time and Energy to Actually Do It

FOREWORD

Imagine for just a moment, motoring down a highway less traveled in rural Mississippi. Farmland spreads out before you and the road unwinds; a house sprinkled here and there, quaint little towns, Spanish moss hanging from huge oak trees, Southern charm, amazing food which drips "finger-lickin' good," down-home tales spun only as true Southerners can spin them. Along the way, you feel joy, grief, pride, prejudice, rejection, exhilaration, jubilation, and triumph.

Imagine growing up within a culture cemented in the constraints of deep-rooted tradition, Bible Belt religion, and great expectation. You've been taught that being "different" is an illness and a sin. Visualize coming out to your family who refuses to accept you or even begin to try to understand you, as they pray for your soul and wrestle with the demons of shame and the fear of being the butt of gossip and scorn.

Now, imagine your fear, anger, and hurt when you are that little girl who is different. You must leave all you have known and loved behind to grow and evolve into your authentic self, seemingly alone and adrift as you try desperately to discover your true path through life.

Elizabeth McCain makes her written debut in this memoir with a timeless collection of stories adapted and expanded from her one-woman play, *A Lesbian Belle Tells…* She takes us on a journey of what it was like to grow up in the deep South, navigating the sometimes stormy, awkward, bizarre, and hilarious waters of Southern culture, ritual, and rites-of-passage. She weaves a tapestry rich with imagery and immense feeling, provoking laughter, tears, and hope as she finds self-acceptance while experiencing the pain of coming out to her family. She then describes the profound joy of finding validation and unconditional love with old and new friends, and meeting and making a life with her soul mate.

Elizabeth's compilation of stories provides a rich narrative for anyone who is struggling or has struggled with rejection and serves as a guide for facing the bold task of becoming who we are meant to be.

Having grown up in Mississippi, and eventually facing my personal truth, Elizabeth's stories resonate with me and remind me of my tribulations and eventual acceptance of myself and growing into my own skin. When I first saw her live show in Rehoboth Beach, I was struck by her willingness to share her intimate adventures, from her scotch drinking Aunt Liber sharing her Delta tales on the porch at their family summer home, called "Southern Comfort," to coming out to the church ladies at her Mama's funeral.

Listening to Elizabeth reminded me of my personal story because I also was reared in a very traditional Southern way. To be isolated, ostracized, and held prisoner by the patriarchy and by the shame of others is a difficult road. The aggression and hatred I endured were palpable and at times terrifying.

Eventually, I, too made my way north to the more open, diverse, progressive culture offered by the burgeoning revolution taking shape in the LGBT community of the Washington, DC metropolitan area in the 1990s. I remember Lammas Women's bookstore, The Mautner Project for lesbians, and the vibrant lesbian bars such as Phase 1, Hung Jury, and the First Saturdays women's dance parties. These places were electric, inviting spaces where I could be myself and where I found my tribe. The personals sections of *The Washington Blade*, the oldest gay newspaper in the U.S., was always a fun read, where likely connections could be perused and pursued long before the advent of the digital age. I, like Elizabeth, was fortunate to have been there to experience it. Many life-long friendships and fond memories were made and will forever be treasured. I evolved socially and politically in DC thanks to the guidance, mentorship and comradery of the incredible sisterhood I found there.

I invite you to come along for the ride and take this journey with Elizabeth as you read this memoir. It will leave its mark on you, as it did me. Sit down, relax, kick off your shoes, and savor every delectable tale spun only as a true lesbian belle can tell.

Jamie Fox,
Producer, DJ, Entertainer, Entrepreneur

INTRODUCTION

"Two or three things I know, two or three things I know for sure, and one of them is that to go on living I have to tell stories, that stories are the one sure way I know to touch the heart and change the world."
- Dorothy Allison

I believe we all long for more story in our lives. A story is a meaningful event with a beginning, middle, and end. It includes what we want, how we struggle, and what we learn. A compelling story has a consequence. The consequence is the change in us.

Story provides medicine for the soul. Our personal narratives reveal how we make sense of our lives and how we connect with one another. When we tell, write, or reframe our stories, a spark ignites in us. Some of the most meaningful times in my life have included sharing and listening to stories. From my Southern childhood spent listening to my Daddy's stories about our hometown's most colorful characters to my flamboyant, scotch sippin' Aunt Liber telling her Mississippi Delta tales on the porch with style and sass, to gathering in lesbian circles sharing our coming out experiences, the power of story has always comforted me, entertained me, and healed me back into belonging.

We are living in divisive and challenging times. Since the presidential election of 2016, our legal rights as LGBTQ+ people are being threatened and destroyed. Old fears and memories of being judged and shamed are resurfacing. We have lived through a wealth of stories – some heartbreaking, and others empowering. Many of us have suffered through family estrangement, loss, betrayal, discrimination, and sexual assault because of who we love. Many of us have been cast out of religious and spiritual institutions. Some of us have lived through difficult break-ups and divorces. Although these experiences have wounded us, I believe that we are resilient people. When we share our written and spoken stories with one another, we feel our strength and solidarity together as a community. We are stronger than we think we are.

Sometimes we need to let go of old stories that no longer serve us–especially the painful ones we are attached to and repeat over and over. Sometimes we need to reframe and reclaim our stories from a higher perspective and tell them from the wisdom of the soul–that eternal spiritual essence we all have, however we name that (God/Goddess/Higher Power/Universe). I invite you to do this in your own way as you are reading this memoir.

I sincerely hope that my stories in this memoir touch your heart and inspire you. Some of these stories are from my one-woman play, *A Lesbian Belle Tells...* which is about my true stories of growing up in a traditional, Christian, Mississippi family, coming out in Washington, DC in the 90s, experiencing family estrangement, and finding love, healing, and belonging. Some of my stories are outrageous and hilarious. Some are intense and painful. Others are heartwarming and tender. I offer you my experiences with the vulnerability and wisdom that come from living through several dark nights of the soul during times of deep grief, despair, and midlife transitions. Many times, I've needed to descend to the underworld of loss only to ascend into living more fully. I've realized this is the cycle of death and rebirth that happens throughout life. I've learned to embrace it all with compassion for myself and others. I'm not perfect, but my life is richer because I'm committed to savoring and reframing my most meaningful and painful stories.

I wrote this memoir from the perspective of a Southern gal on a tenacious quest to find self-acceptance and belonging. The stories to follow convey universal themes of family, coming out, loss, love, forgiveness, and belonging. However, I wrote this book specifically for LGBTQ+ folks of all ages. I trust that whoever you are, if this book has made its way into your hands or onto your screens, you are meant to read it.

I identify as a lesbian rather than queer because this is the orientation I know, love, and have fought hard to keep. I understand that many people within our LGBTQ+ culture identify as queer. I believe there is room for all of us at the table - however we choose to identify. I also describe myself as a progressive, middle-aged, trailblazing, Southern "lipstick lesbian." I will forever remain a consciously recovering Southern belle from a long line of unrecovered belles, bless their hearts!

So settle in, get cozy, and travel with me through my story adventures during various seasons of my life. Roll with them, laugh with them, and allow them to spark memories of your own stories. Honor the stories which reside in your heart and mind. I encourage you to share your stories of coming out, loss, healing, and celebration, as well as triumph over tragedy within your family, your community, and beyond. For I believe that your stories provide you with the best medicine to heal just about anything.

Note: Some names in this book have been changed for the sake of privacy.

CHAPTER 1

Becoming a Lesbian

How many lesbians can thank an old boyfriend for helping them come out? I raise my hand to David, the first person to help me consider switching teams and venturing into lesbian-land.

David was a cute, witty, slightly sarcastic, political, liberal, twenty-nine year-old social worker. Originally from Pittsburgh - but with New Orleans roots on his mother's side - I loved his understanding and appreciation of the eccentricities of Southern culture; our slower pace of savoring life with storytelling on the porch, appreciating the short stories of Eudora Welty, and our art of throwing a damn good party right after a Southern funeral.

I'd fallen for David after only a few months of dating. We'd met at a progressive Episcopal church on Capitol Hill in Washington, DC. We were in an intense twelve-week confirmation class in 1991. This was not your Mama's confirmation class. There was not much focus on Jesus or the Bible. I remember lots of small group discussions and skits about community and belonging. It felt like a cross between sloppy group therapy and an encounter group from the 70s. David caught my eye in the first class, with his dark, wavy hair with a touch of grey and his dark, brown eyes which were very alluring. We spent hours laughing and telling stories about our dysfunctional families. When the confirmation class ended, we had already established a good friendship, so we started dating. David was the only guy I had dated who had already been in individual and group therapy for several years. His quest for understanding and healing of his family-of-origin wounds impressed me. I had also begun a journey in psychotherapy and was committed to my spiritual growth. I had dated a lot of Southern good ol' boys, as well as a few Northern guys, who didn't have a bit of self-awareness or curiosity about their childhoods and family dynamics. I called those guys "bad boy Bubbas." They were handsome, rich, and hot–but unconscious, uninteresting, and definitely not intellectual enough for me.

David readily admitted he was not good at relationships because of his commitment issues. It took me a while to see it and believe him. However, I gradually found it hiding beneath his charm and intellect. As writer Maya Angelou wisely stated, "When someone shows you who they are, believe them the first time."

Sadly, after a few months of dating, I began to suspect David was seeing his former girlfriend again, who was also in our confirmation class. He was vague about his weekend plans and seemed withdrawn. I guess deep down, I knew he wasn't emotionally available, but I was crazy about him and hoped I could make him forget about her. (Clearly, I hadn't had enough therapy or read enough books on co-dependency.)

One night, I pranced into David's tiny, modern, Capitol Hill apartment with a bold plan. I went into his bathroom and took off my Burberry trench coat, jeans, and black cashmere sweater. I stripped off all my clothes and pulled my playful purple boa out of my backpack. I quickly threw it around my neck and proudly strutted naked into the living room where David sat reading *The Washington Post*. He looked up from the newspaper when I snatched it away from him. Then I sat in his lap and leaned into him for a kiss. He interrupted this seductive moment to utter these fateful words, "Elizabeth, have you ever considered becoming a lesbian?"

What the hell? This was my seduction ploy, and he killed the moment. At first, I was stunned and outraged. A lesbian? I didn't think I was homophobic, but I had never been aware of being sexually attracted to women. Nor had I ever had a man suggest this to me. I mean, David and I had enjoyed many passionate nights together. I couldn't understand where his question was coming from – unless he was avoiding commitment. What a way to create some distraction and drama.

In a stern tone of voice, I replied, "David, there you go again, trying to push me away! You need to go back to therapy."

"Come on, Elizabeth, straight men are dogs. We just want one thing from women. We're simple. But women are amazing! And you're a feminist. You love those weird Goddess circles and women's dinner parties. If you want, I can introduce you to some cool feminist lesbians."

His response was over the top. I was confused and furious all at once. "David, I did not grow up having crushes on my P.E. teachers!" I stormed out of his apartment–after I put on some clothes, of course.

As I drove home that night, I pondered David's questions. Was I unconsciously attracted to women? Was David picking up on something I had buried? Could I be bisexual? Most importantly, I wondered if becoming a lesbian was a viable option. I had to admit, this idea sort of intrigued me.

The next week, I took these issues to my therapist and told her about David's question. Lynne was an open-minded, compassionate, middle-aged, pastoral counselor. She was my first psychotherapist, whom I saw for several years. In a gentle and soothing way, Lynne suggested I embrace my "not knowing" and have fun exploring my sexuality. Her acceptance and encouragement were just what I needed.

I confronted David with my suspicions that he was still seeing his old girlfriend. When he finally admitted he was, I promptly ended the relationship. I was angry and hurt for a while, especially when I had to endure seeing David and his new/old girlfriend at church.

A few months after the break-up, I became friends with a woman named Sherry at a women's counseling center, where I worked as a new psychotherapist. Sherry was taking a break from her corporate career and volunteering at this women's center. Her short, blonde, spiky hair and piercing, aqua-colored eyes gave her an enticing, edgy look. She was a hot, thirty-six-year-old, about seven years my senior. What really fascinated me was that Sherry was a Berkeley, California, Birkenstock-wearing, braless feminist.

One day, Sherry invited me to lunch. She mentioned she was interested in exploring the possibility of going to graduate school to become a therapist and wanted to discuss this with me. We had an engaging, three-hour lunch at the Wolftrap Deli in Vienna, Virginia, where we talked about all kinds of things–from our experiences with our therapists, to our love for Goddess spirituality, feminist psychology, and liberal politics. We discovered we were both reading the same book by Clarissa Pinkola Estés, *Women Who Run with the Wolves*, which explores various cultural perspectives and stories about the wild woman archetype. Needless to say, I was spellbound and mesmerized by this woman who was so willing to discuss our many similar interests.

Somehow, we never got around to discussing her interest in graduate school. It was impossible to ignore the mutual spark growing between us, like two teenaged girls beginning an exciting new friendship.

I confided to Sherry about my break-up with David. "Oh Sherry, I recently broke up with my boyfriend, David. And he asked me the oddest thing. He asked me if I'd ever thought of becoming... a lesbian!"

She replied in her velvety, Lauren Bacall voice, "Well, have you, Elizabeth?"

With a wildly beating heart and sweat dripping down my back, I proclaimed, "Oh, God, well, no. I mean, I love women in that *Steel Magnolias* kind of way, but I'm still attracted to guys."

There was a pregnant pause. "Hmmm..." was all Sherry said.

We continued to get together for long lunches. Slowly, I felt my attraction to her growing, but I wasn't sure what to do about it. I'd never felt this kind of attraction with men. I mean, I had been sexually attracted to men, but I had never felt connected in the deep, emotional way I felt with Sherry. I felt like I was falling in love with a close friend. It was more than a crush. The forbidden lesbian element was also alluring. I didn't know any lesbians. I'd been to the Lesbian and Gay March on Washington with some of my straight women friends who worked at Planned Parenthood. They introduced me to their friends, who were cute lesbians with short, butch haircuts wearing Dr. Martens. I remember admiring their courage in strutting with such confidence.

My friendship with Sherry quickly deepened since I saw her at the women's center three days a week. We had several more lunches and almost daily phone calls. This was several years before cell phones and texting, back when people still talked to each other on the phone. Answering machines were all we had to remind us of missed calls.

One night, I went to Sherry's house for dinner and a movie. She greeted me at the door wearing a UC Berkeley sweatshirt, red-tagged Levi's, and brown cowboy boots. After a simple supper of chicken curry soup and salad, we went to her living room. Sherry suggested we watch a lesbian movie, the classic *Desert Hearts*. (Little did I know that this was many-a-lesbian's seduction tactic.) If you are a lesbian over forty and have been out for at least fifteen years, you've probably seen this film. And if you haven't seen it, watch it! It's about a middle-aged professor who falls in love with a younger woman on a ranch in the 1950s. As we watched this movie, I felt turned on by the erotic love-making between the two beautiful women on screen. (The scene in the hotel is especially sensual and hot). In the middle of the hotel scene, Sherry scooted in close to me while I was engaged in the action on the screen. The sexual tension was building between the two of us, and the cats must have felt it too. They circled the couch, crying out, "Meow... meeoww."

As two women started making love in that hot hotel scene with writhing and tender caresses, I heard, "I so wanna kiss you, Elizabeth."

All at once, I felt a combination of thrill and terror. The possibility of kissing this sexy, butch lesbian was both enticing and taboo. Actually, Sherry had a compelling combination of butch and femme energy. She expressed her butch side in her rugged fashion sense, and her femme side by wearing tiny gold hoop earrings and a hint of rose-tinted lip gloss. I felt her breath exhaling onto my neck, and my heart was pounding with desire and fear.

What will it mean if I kiss a woman? I thought. Will this make me a lesbian? Or am I bisexual? And what would my conventional Mississippi family think? My worries began to fade as I felt my curiosity growing about what it would feel like to kiss a woman, this particular woman, who I found so hard to resist.

The next moment, Sherry pounced and laid one on me. I closed my eyes and told myself I could pretend this was a man. When her soft lips met mine, and I touched her chiseled cheekbones, I felt in that

moment like I had come home. Sherry was soft and curvy. I felt safe
with her. Her scent of patchouli with a touch of jasmine intoxicated
me. This was no man! I loved kissing her maybe because I had never
felt this sensual before–as a woman kissing another woman. A bolt
of hot desire shot through every cell in my body.

Then, like a lesbian Rhett Butler, Sherry lifted me into her strong,
butch arms and carried me up the stairs to her bedroom. I remember
her walls were painted a soft lavender, and her sheets were deep
purple satin. There was a Three Graces print on the wall, and I noticed
familiar books on her bedside table, *A Return to Love* by Marianne
Williamson and *Goddesses in Everywoman* by Jean Shinoda Bolen.

Sherry laid me down on her bed and ripped her clothes off. It
was dark in her bedroom, but I could see the outline of her body.
She was a full-figured, large-breasted, Botticelli-shaped woman.
Mercilessly, I took off my cashmere sweater and black bra.

Sherry climbed on top of me and whispered, "What cha want, girl?"

"Oh, I don't know, Sherry. I don't even know what lesbians do.
Just take me!"

And she did. Sherry touched me in places and in ways no man
ever had. Breast to breast, hip to hip, an unleashing of passion
began. I felt drunk with desire, intimidated, and awkward, like I
was a naive virgin all over again. I had slept with several guys in
my twenties and considered myself reasonably sexually experienced
and confident. But sleeping with a woman was new and different.
There were no rules. Or were there lesbian rules or guidelines for a
first time? I was woefully ignorant and embarrassed. And let's say
I was not sexually assertive with Sherry. As soon as I started to feel
pleasure, I felt fear and guilt.

Eventually, she wanted me to make love to her, but I couldn't. I
told her I wasn't ready. In my mind, I heard a voice saying, "If you
make love to her, that means you're at least bisexual or a lesbian,

and this could mess up your life. I mean, what would your family think?" My homophobic Southern self was not about to consider any alternative sexual plan.

Sherry expressed her disappointment and assured me it was okay. "As you get more comfortable with your sexuality, it will probably be a natural thing for you to make love to a woman. That is, if you're a real lesbian. Are you? Or do you think you're bi? Do you know which identity feels right?"

I didn't know what to say. I didn't want to sound confused and freaked out on the first steamy night of sexual discovery.

"Well, Sherry, I don't know. This is all so new to me. I've never thought about being sexual with a woman. I mean, I've admired lesbians from afar–like when I marched in the Lesbian and Gay March in DC last spring. Those lesbians looked cool, confident, and brave."

Sherry calmly replied, "Well, take your time. We'll go slowly. Let's get to know each other. I'm a bit hesitant because there's a possibility you might go back to men if you're bi. And I don't have the energy to bring a woman out of the closet. That's a huge job, and you'll need a lot of therapy and support."

"Right, Sherry. I understand. Thanks. I probably am bisexual, but I'm not sure. I hope that's okay."

Sherry sighed deeply and seemed hesitant. "We'll take this one day at a time. That's the way I live my life. I've told you, I'm in a twelve-step program, AA. I've been sober for ten years."

"Yeah, right. I'm so glad you're sober. I love the twelve steps. Cool. We'll take this one day at a time."

For the rest of the night, we held each other. I didn't get any sleep.

I had to leave Sherry's house by 8:00 am to make it to choir rehearsal at my church in DC by 10:00 am. I thanked her for our evening together. "I had a wonderful evening with you. Let's talk in a few days and have dinner again next weekend."

Sherry's only reply was, "We'll see."

I managed to make it to my condo to shower and dress for church. I was only a few minutes late for choir rehearsal at St. Mark's Episcopal Church on Capitol Hill. I breathed a sigh of relief and walked into the church. I remember wondering if anyone noticed the look of guilt on my face. I felt as if I were wearing a scarlet "L" on my forehead. Worrying about what people thought about me has always been a part of my nature–a Southern thing I learned from my mother, who learned it from her mother, and it goes on and on. An unspoken rule among heterosexual, Christian, Southern women dictates they must be a combination of pretty and proper as well as sexy and seductive–a paradox I've always hated. I'd already spent several years in therapy working on letting go of my guilt and shame around losing my virginity in college and being on the pill for several years. Like most Southern Mamas in the 1970s and 80s, mine was overly religious, submissive to the patriarchal culture, old school traditional, and unable to talk about sexuality.

In my choir, I'd become close friends with another soprano named Laura. I'd previously confided to her I had a crush on an older butch lesbian. Although Laura was engaged to a man, she told me she'd had a lesbian relationship with a girl when she was in high school. Laura had described it as a "delicious affair," but she knew she wanted to marry a man and have children. It was a short-lived fling for her. I was grateful that Laura told me her lesbian story because this gave me the support and validation I needed. Laura was feminine and mainstream-looking, like me. Her story permitted me to keep exploring with Sherry.

That morning when I sat next to Laura in the choir, she whispered to me, "Oh My God, you slept with her, didn't you? I can see it in your eyes!"

I smiled, gave her a wink, and said, "Let's have brunch after church, and I'll tell you the whole story."

I was relieved and delighted to tell Laura everything about the night before with Sherry. "Oh, Laura. It was quite an evening! I felt such a combination of things—longing, desire, fear, confusion, and guilt. It felt very sensual and spiritual." I described the cats circling us on Sherry's couch and the whole lesbian Rhett Butler seduction scene. We howled with laughter.

"There's nothing like being made love to by another woman... cuz she knows your body," Laura told me. "That's the embodiment of the Divine Feminine. If you have homophobic thoughts, shift your thinking and have fun with this! You don't have to know where it's going. And you don't have to know if you're lesbian or bisexual. Go with the flow." Laura paused and then said, "God, I miss the sex I had with Jill ten years ago. There's never been such passion in my life since then."

For about six weeks, I had long romantic lunches and dinners with Sherry. She wanted me to meet her lesbian friends in AA (out of respect for her years of sobriety, I never drank around her), but I wasn't ready to meet her friends. Only my therapist, spiritual director, and Laura knew I was dating Sherry. Even saying those words "dating Sherry" was challenging for me. I had never imagined I would date a woman. On the other hand, I never had that dream of getting married to a man and having children that most of my friends shared growing up. I'd had one long-term boyfriend my senior year in college for about three years. I knew we were incompatible. I broke up with him several times in the last six months of our relationship. Then, for the next six years, I had several short-term relationships with guys. Although the sex with men was okay, I never felt like I had a satisfying emotional connection with any men I dated. Most of my needs for emotional intimacy were met through friendships with women, all of whom were heterosexual, as far as I knew.

Sherry and I didn't last long. She was bipolar. During one of her depressive episodes, she disappeared on me for about ten days. During this time, a guy named Ron called me and asked me out. We'd met at a conference for psychotherapists the year before. We had almost dated, but he was ending a relationship back then. Ron was a cute, Southern, tall, smart, red-headed guy who played the guitar and sang. So here he was calling me a year later when I was in my first lesbian relationship. I was torn. On the one hand, I remembered how cute he was. I loved his South Georgia accent. And I thought it would be cool to date another therapist. On the other hand, I cared about Sherry and was attached to her. But her depressive episodes were becoming more frequent and lasted longer each time. I knew it would be easier to date a guy. I knew the heterosexual roles, and it was what my family and my culture expected from me. I was tired of keeping my lesbian secret from my family, especially from my mother, to whom I'd always felt close.

I decided to be honest and tell Sherry I wanted to date Ron. I told her I thought I was bisexual, and it was easier to date guys. I knew she would be upset, but I wasn't quite ready for her response.

"I knew you'd go back to men. You bisexual women are all alike. You are all traitors who break our lesbian hearts."

Sherry stormed out of the restaurant where we were having dinner, which stunned me. I continued to see her at work for the next few months, which was awkward. Much of the time, she ignored me. A few months later, Sherry left the women's center to go back to corporate work, and we lost touch. Although I was sad to lose her, I was relieved.

Ron and I had a few dates. I was definitely attracted to him and felt that Southern connection with him. He seemed open-minded and progressive until the day I realized he was not. I remember the exact moment. We were on our third date leaving the National Gallery on a bitterly cold Saturday in February. As we walked down the sidewalk on our way to his Chevy truck, we passed a lesbian couple holding hands.

Ron snickered and said, "Those girls need a good man. They don't know what they're missing."

I was horrified by his reaction. I immediately confronted Ron and said, "You didn't just say that, did you, Ron? Are you judging my lesbian sisters? That was a very homophobic remark you made."

"Lesbian sisters? Is there something you've neglected to tell me, Elizabeth? I know you are a feminist. So, um, does that also make you a lesbian?"

I decided to take a risk and tell him the truth. "Well, Ron, I have slept with one woman, rather recently. So, I'm probably bisexual. But even if I were straight, your homophobic remark would still offend me. I thought you were different from most straight men, but I guess you are threatened by lesbians."

We discussed this over dinner, then we went back to his apartment. Things started to get romantic, but there was an awkward tension. He played the guitar and sang "A Bridge Over Troubled Water." We started to make out. Then, suddenly, he stopped kissing me and said, "I'm sorry, Elizabeth. I keep thinking about you being with a woman and the bisexual thing. This just won't work for me. I need to be with a woman who is absolutely, positively heterosexual."

We agreed to stop dating. I was sad but knew this was the right thing to do.

You might be wondering what happened to Sherry.

Four years later, I was on the Mall in DC, looking at the AIDS quilt (with another girlfriend). From a distance, I thought I saw

Sherry. She looked the same except her hair was no longer spiky and short. It was shoulder-length, which gave her a more feminine look. I walked over to her.

"Hey, Sherry. It's great to see you!" I said.

Her only response was, "There's just one thing I wanna know: are you lesbian or bisexual?"

I smiled and winked at her and said, "Wouldn't you love to know?"

CHAPTER 2

Bisexual Potluck

For more than a year, I struggled with my sexual orientation. Was I bisexual or lesbian? I had been somewhat attracted to men and had several relationships with them. I'd only been truly in love with one man and he was emotionally unavailable. The sex had been okay, but not fabulous. I loved the kissing and heavy petting. But I could do without the penetration. I thought penises were awkward and odd-looking. All the guys I'd slept with were focused on sex that was fast and devoid of tenderness. They were focused on getting off as soon as possible. Then they'd roll over and go to sleep or get up and smoke a cigarette. I appreciated handsome men and muscular physiques, but more from an aesthetic perspective rather than a sexual one. I hated that they seemed uncomfortable with my intense emotions.

Women were amazing. The ones I'd allowed myself to be attracted to in those early days of coming out were sexy, bold, athletic, and emotionally complicated. I loved how sensual and confident lesbians were–especially those soft-butch lesbians. The ones I was attracted to also had similar characteristics. They were smart, successful, handsome women with short hair and chiseled cheeks, who also had curvy bodies. My first two girlfriends were very spiritual, which I thought was so hot. To me, there was nothing sexier than talking about the Divine Feminine, the Goddess, meditation, and Mary Oliver's poetry. But was I a lesbian? Was I ready to give up my privilege as a heterosexual woman?

Of even greater concern to me was acceptance by my family, especially my mother and sister. How would they react if I embraced this new lesbian identity? Generations of Southern women in my family had bonded around having husbands with nice homes and children. There was acceptance, celebration, and respect that women received in my family when they married a man and gained immediate entry into the "respectable Southern lady" club. One could not escape those awful rituals of bridesmaids' luncheons, engagement parties, choosing china patterns, a white wedding dress, and wedding food. I'd been to several weddings. In fact, I was my childhood best friend's maid of honor in her traditional wedding in Aberdeen, Mississippi. I hated every detail of the process–from wearing the hideous light pink, scratchy taffeta dress to the boring, polite conversations and fuss over the status-symbol gifts of silver trays, cookbooks, and lingerie. I hated pretending this was fun. I had no desire to marry a man at twenty-three. And the odd thing is, I didn't share the dream of getting married that most Southern heterosexual girls dreamed. I never wanted children. When my childhood friends got married throughout my twenties, I felt like I was losing these friends to a tribe I would never be in. I knew I wanted to be in love and thought I wanted a career as an actress. I thought marriage to a man and having a family would attach me to an oppressive patriarchal system. I identified as a feminist since I was twenty-one when the feminist writer, Betty

Friedan came to speak at my college, Randolph-Macon Woman's College. Thanks to her riveting speech on feminism and women's equality, I learned that feminism was not the evil, man-hating concept Mama talked about.

I knew our homophobic, heterosexist culture perceived lesbians as perverse, angry, man-hating, unattractive women. Even though it was clear those were false, ridiculous stereotypes, I had internalized them. So, considering dating women in my twenties was nowhere in my consciousness.

And then there was the conservative Christian theology about homosexuality being a sin. According to a narrow hetero-normative interpretation of the Bible, marriage was considered a holy union that was only between a man and a woman. Understanding the Bible was written by a group of Middle Eastern men centuries ago, it isn't surprising that this limited view also holds that a woman must save herself for her husband and hold on to her virginity until marriage. I always thought this was a load of crap. A wise, feminist, spiritual director helped me let go of these beliefs. I read an insightful book *What the Bible Really Says About Homosexuality*, by Daniel A. Helminiak, which goes through all the passages in the Bible commonly interpreted as condemning homosexuality. In this book, scholars explain these interpretations are about faulty translation, poor interpretation, and patriarchal, Middle Eastern culture.

I remember spouting off to Mama as a teenager when she lectured me about being a virgin until I married. I said something like,

"That's ridiculous. I mean, what if I never marry? Or what if I don't marry 'til I'm forty? I'm not gonna be a prude and save myself for some man. Men don't save their purity for women. If I love someone and am in a committed relationship, I'll sleep with him."

Mama gasped, and said, "I'm shocked by your rebellious attitude, and so is Jesus!"

I continued to rant, "This virginity thing is overrated. And so is Christianity. Maybe I'll become Buddhist, or Pagan, or maybe I'll convert to Judaism. Christianity is a patriarchal religion with the long-term exclusion of women from leadership and sexist language. My image of God is not masculine. I prefer the Divine Feminine, known as the Goddess."

Needless to say, Mama was horrified.

Identifying as bisexual was easier for me than identifying as lesbian because it gave me the option of going back to men if I wanted to. What exactly did that mean? One day, I'd desire men and the next day, I'd desire women? Did being bisexual mean I was equally attracted to men and women? Or was this part of my gradual movement into accepting myself as a lesbian?

To answer some of these questions, I decided it was time to explore an ad I found in the *Washington Blade*, the gay newspaper in DC, for a women's bisexual potluck and spiritual circle. It was way out in rural Virginia, past Manassas, which was conservative country just outside of the DC area. I knew I wanted to go.

I called the number in the ad for the potluck. I was shaking as I said in an almost whisper, "Hi. My name's Elizabeth. I'm calling about the um… bisexual women's potluck?"

"Oh, hi, Elizabeth. I'm Sapphire Moonstone. We'd love to have you at our potluck. We also have a Goddess circle and practice Wiccan magic. We'd love to have you, dear. Please, come!"

"Thank you, Sapphire! I'd love to! See you Saturday night."

So, on a rainy summer Saturday night, I got up my nerve and went to the potluck carrying a delicious red velvet cake. After all, one does need to contribute to a bisexual potluck. I arrived at a small Cape Cod house and was greeted by an extroverted, round, pretty woman in a tie-dye dress with a pink, lavender and green mermaid tattoo, and the most enormous bosoms I'd ever seen.

With a twinkle in her eyes, she said, "Hi, Elizabeth. I'm Sapphire Moonstone. Welcome! Come on in, and I'll introduce you to our tribe."

A group of young, slightly feminine looking women was gathered in a circle. Most of them were wearing long, flowing, hippy skirts and sexy silver and bronze sandals. They were all curvy, pretty, and welcoming.

I discovered Sapphire was actually a High Priestess of the Dianic Tradition of Feminist Wicca. (To those who might be wondering, the Dianic Wiccan tradition is a Neo-Pagan religion which honors only the Divine Feminine, also called the Goddess.) I'd arrived as they were about to start their ritual. Sapphire called in the four directions and invoked the Goddess.

Together we sang this magical chant by Lindie Lila,

> *We all come from the Goddess,*
> *And to her we shall return,*
> *Like a drop of rain,*
> *Flowing to the ocean.*

I was starting to feel at home–like I'd found my tribe of spiritual soul sisters. Goddess spirituality had been my path for the past couple of years since I left the Episcopal church. Then, Sapphire's friend, Rubyfruit, made an announcement. Rubyfruit looked like Sapphire's twin, except a bit rounder with flaming red hair and a nose piercing.

She got this kind of naughty look on her face and said, "Elizabeth, we want to welcome you and initiate you as our new sister into our coven. We focus on blessing one another's naked bodies."

"Oh, well, thank you, Rubyfruit. What is the focus of your circle?" (I was getting nervous and skeptical.) I was open to embracing the bisexual identity and being in a coven, but I was not comfortable with public nudity.

"Well, you see, Elizabeth, in our coven, the focus is honoring the Goddess as she relates to our sexuality. Some of us have girlfriends.

And some of us have husbands and/or boyfriends. There's no place for us bi babes in the lesbian and gay culture. So, we bless one another's naked bodies. Then our men join us, and we do tantric breathwork and have consensual sex play. We're integrating our sexuality with our spirituality. We have all kinds of sex toys. If you're not comfortable joining us, you can watch. It will be hot!"

I was stunned. It sounded like their coven was some kind of bisexual orgy. Compared to most Southern women, I was fairly open-minded sexually, but I knew I had no desire to join them in their sex play session. Goddess have mercy, I thought. If my Mississippi Mama could see me now!

Luckily, I think fast on my feet. I handed Rubyfruit my homemade red velvet cake.

"Thank you, ladies, but I have a darling new dachshund puppy at home. Gotta run, but keep the cake!"

And I ran out of that house as fast as I could and drove home in a nervous burst of energy. It was amazing I made it home in one piece. I was entirely confused. Was I bisexual or lesbian? I knew I was past the sexually adventurous stage. I wondered if I even needed to label myself, but I knew I longed to belong to a group of women who loved women, whether they thought they were born gay or chose it. At this point, I felt like I was more attracted to women than men. I thought the lesbian identity might be a better fit for me.

This was 1994. In some ways, it was a simpler time in terms of sexual orientation. We weren't yet using words like non-binary, queer, and pansexual. Our dominant identities were lesbian, gay, or bisexual. (Transgender, crossdressers, and transsexual people were beginning to come out in the DC area, but they didn't yet have a political movement.)

I read every book on coming out, and on gay and lesbian spirituality and sexuality I could find. Helpful ones were *Lesbian Sex* by JoAnn Loulan, *Coming Out Spiritually* by Christian de la Huerta, *Positively Gay, Setting Them Straight,* and *Permanent Partners,* all by Betty Berzon.

I pondered how I might weave my way into the lesbian community. I felt excited and intimidated being around lesbians. I was aware that I was still straight-looking. I knew I had the "privilege" of passing as a heterosexual because I looked mainstream and feminine, even when I cut my hair short. I briefly explored dressing in a more crunchy, hippy way, wearing long flowing skirts, and sometimes tie-dye t-shirts. I thought about getting a tattoo, but that would be permanent. I also had my career as a psychotherapist to consider. Most of my clients and therapist colleagues were mainstream, suburban, heterosexual women I knew through association with the women's counseling center where I worked.

While I was starting to feel more comfortable with my sexuality in Washington, DC, where I had lived for seven years, my Southern past haunted me with reminders of my conservative Christian family. Wait until you read about where and how I grew up.

CHAPTER 3

Southern Roots Through Story

B efore I tell you about my coming out process with my family-of-origin, I'd like to give you a taste of my very traditional, Southern childhood. I grew up with older parents who doted on me as their baby girl. I was their surprise, born when Mama was thirty-eight and Daddy was forty-three. They'd already had two sons, Jem and Reynolds, seventeen and twelve when I was born, and one daughter, Marguerite, who was nine. My childhood was steeped in story. Daddy was my greatest storytelling teacher. He was always telling tales about his family and local characters in our tiny town of 2,800 people.

"Did I tell you about your great uncle Bob who was killed when a train hit his car and they found a young woman (who wasn't his wife) sitting in his dead lap?" His stories exuded Southern Gothic drama, an element in literature that includes dark humor, freakishness, and often delusional characters.

After Daddy came home from working at the bank, he would often start a story like this, "Lord have mercy, girl! Annie Mae, who works down at the plant on Highway 45 has shot her third husband, and he deserved it!"

On and on his stories went.

Daddy came from a long line of storytelling farmers, small business owners, and a few preachers. His family was from "the hills" in Webster county, in Mississippi, near a tiny town called Eupora, roughly two hours north and slightly east of Jackson, the state's capital. His father, my grandfather, James Everett McCain Sr., moved to Okolona, a railroad town roughly 50 miles north and east of Eupora, in 1930 to work at the Bank of Okolona. (This bank was the first small, privately owned bank in Mississippi to open after the crash of 1929.) As soon as the bank was incorporated, they selected my grandfather to become the president.

A few years before I was born, Daddy became president of the bank after his father died in 1960. He wore gray and black suits that rarely matched, fedoras he'd owned since the 1950s, and black and white wing-tipped shoes to work. He was overweight and tired-looking by the time I was six, and he was forty-nine. As a younger man, Daddy was a very trim, handsome man with a thick head of dark brown hair and sparkling, celery-green eyes. He still thought of himself as a handsome young man. In his 50's, he looked into the mirror every morning of my childhood, and he'd say to himself, "James Everett McCain, you're still a good-looking man!"

Then, he'd look at me and say, "Elizabeth, you're such a lucky girl to have such a pretty mama, and a handsome, successful daddy."

Even as an eight-year-old, I'd roll my eyes.

Then Daddy would sing Gershwin's "Summertime" to me, with slightly changed lyrics:

> *Summertime, and the living is easy.*
> *Fish are jumpin, and the cotton is high,*
> *Oh, your daddy's rich, and your mama's good looking,*
> *So, hush, little Lizbuth, don't you cry.*

I loved it when Daddy told me the story of my birth.

"Yeah, honey. When you were born, I remember being in the waiting room at the hospital with all the other daddies. The nurse came in to tell me that we have the most delicate baby she'd ever seen. When I called your grandmother and your sister to tell them you were a girl, they danced around the house!"

Although most of Daddy's stories were entertaining and funny, the ones I enjoyed the most were the ones in which he made himself vulnerable. He'd start a story about how strict his father was and how hard it was to work for him at the bank. Then there would be a poignant pause, and he'd say how much he missed his dad and how he felt guilty for being a difficult son.

He explained, "Elizabeth, your granddaddy and I clashed. He was a perfectionist and I'm a procrastinator. He was introverted and I'm extroverted. And he was a mystery, and I'm fairly simple. He died suddenly from a heart attack in my arms in the barbershop one afternoon. That was the only time I told him I loved him. I've always regretted that. I wish I'd appreciated my Daddy more."

I wondered if this was Daddy's way of hinting for me to appreciate him more.

His occasional vulnerability helped me feel close to him. It didn't happen often, because Daddy was more content with making people laugh than cry.

Daddy enjoyed people from all walks of life. I remember that he often had two-hour lunches at Mildred's Café, where the local businessmen, farmers, and factory workers all gathered. Besides telling his own stories, Daddy had a natural curiosity about people. When people went to talk to him about getting a loan, it was not uncommon for the meeting to extend into a social visit. Daddy asked folks all about their family and friends. Some would say he had poor boundaries. He was an extrovert off the chart. Connecting with people made him come alive. I can relate to this.

Sometimes in the late afternoons, in my early teens and twenties, Daddy would ask me if I wanted to ride with him in his pickup truck to his farmland and look at his crops of soybeans. As a child, I wasn't very interested in this, but as a young woman, our rides out to Daddy's farmland became our special ritual. It was the only time we spent together without Mama around. Sometimes he offered me a cigarette, from his pack of Marlborough Lights, carefully hidden in the glove compartment.

"Hey, baby, don't tell your Mama. Let's have a smoke and talk about life. Of everyone in the family, you and I are most alike. We're interested in peoples' stories. And we know how to speak up and say what's on our minds. But sometimes we regret what we say."

And then he laughed a deep bass, hearty laugh. I'd smile—partly proud and somewhat stunned that I might have some of his charming and slightly self-centered personality.

Several times a year, when I came home from school, we'd connect and ride all over Chickasaw County, in northeast Mississippi, where Daddy owned several thousand acres of soybeans. He'd point to the right and then left and say,

"Baby girl, see all that land way out to the horizon? That's McCain land. Your granddaddy bought the first tract of land that we call The Taft land because your granddaddy bought some land from President Taft's nephew back in 1930. Land is a very valuable thing to have. You know you're connected to the earth in a powerful way when you own land. You appreciate the changing seasons. You notice death and birth."

Then Daddy took me to see his exotic black swans out on his lake.

"Look at how graceful they are as they glide across the water. It's good to remember to be at ease with life and glide through the waters."

I recently read somewhere that black swans represent the healing powers of love and romance. I realize that Daddy's sense of spirituality was connected to nature–the earth, the seasons, and the beauty of creatures such as swans, geese, and ducks.

Daddy's obsession with me finding a man and marrying well frustrated me. He didn't seem interested in my academic experiences in college. The only questions he asked me were about meeting men. I didn't have a serious boyfriend until I was a senior in college. That relationship was the longest one I had with a guy and only lasted for a couple of years. I often felt judged and not taken seriously by Daddy as a young woman.

While Daddy was extroverted, generous, and charming, he was also prone to depression and anger. He would lash out at Mama if supper wasn't ready when he was hungry. And he was always hungry. I only remember Daddy as overweight and sedentary. He shoveled in food as fast as he could. I remember being embarrassed about his eating at the dinner table when my friends came over to spend the night.

Daddy was a classic food addict–always trying to fill his emptiness inside by overeating. I think he was starved for love and attention because he grew up with an emotionally distant mother and a perfectionist father; he married a woman who was also emotionally distant.

My parents married after only knowing one another for five months. They met at a fraternity party dance at Ole Miss in January, 1946, when Mama was a senior, and Daddy was an alumnus visiting for the weekend. They began a long-distance relationship. Daddy was twenty-five, working at a bank in Tupelo, about an hour from the Ole Miss campus. Mama was a very glamorous, shy, naive, sweet twenty-one-year-old. Daddy said he saw her, asked her to dance with him, and quickly told her he wanted to marry her. They married only a few weeks after Mama graduated from Ole Miss (with her degree in home economics). They had gone to spend the weekend with friends in Arkansas. Mama was supposed to move to Atlanta the next week to start working as a stewardess (as flight attendants were called back then) for Delta. On the drive back from Little Rock, after an argument, Daddy convinced Mama not to take the job, but to marry him instead. They turned around, went back to their friends' house and were married that afternoon by a Methodist minister. They called their parents that night to tell them they were married. Their parents were surprised and disappointed that they didn't have a big, Baptist wedding.

Unfortunately, they had a difficult marriage and were not a compatible couple. They were absolute opposites. Daddy was a restless extrovert and Mama was a reserved introvert. Daddy could be angry, blaming, and demanding. Mama was sometimes emotionally detached and passive-aggressive. He was a typical Southern man of his generation who believed women should be submissive to their husbands. As most upper-middle-class women of her generation, Mama was a traditional housewife and mother. She worked for only one year as a sixth-grade teacher when I was in the first grade. Unfortunately, she had difficulty confronting her husband's verbal abuse.

Mama was an attentive and loving mother. She nurtured me, comforted me, and made me feel special as a little girl. We enjoyed shopping and traveling together when I was a teenager. We shared adventures on tours to California, the Grand Canyon, and Europe. Since my older siblings left home for boarding school and college by the time I was six, Mama had more time to spend with me. As a result, we became close in a way that wasn't possible for my siblings. We were like two separate families.

That also meant Mama put too much of her focus on me to distract herself from her angry, domineering husband. Remember, Mama was thirty-eight when she had me. Today that's not unusual, but in 1963 in rural Mississippi, it was very odd.

I felt self-conscious about having older parents, especially about having an older-looking mother. Most of my friends' parents were ten or fifteen years younger than mine. While other mothers wore their summer shorts and halter tops with shag haircuts and sexy sandals, my Mama wore long, wrap-around skirts popular in the 1970s, with high-necked blouses, sensible shoes, and support hose. Her hair was teased and frosted, which looked like a yellow helmet on her head. She always wore her signature Revlon ruby red lipstick, and a silver Celtic cross. She was a very pretty, middle-aged woman, but she looked more like my grandmother than my mother.

When my parents were in their fifties, they traveled a great deal with their younger, adventurous friends, Bob and Emily Henson, and their bachelor pal, Mike Malski, who was a thirty-three-year-old attorney. When they went on long international trips to Mexico, India, and Afghanistan, I stayed with Grandmother, Daddy's mother, Gertrude Pinson McCain, who lived around the corner from our house. I loved going to her house because it was older than ours. It was a charming brick Cape Cod house, built around 1920. The house had high ceilings, a sun porch, and a formal living room that was only used when she hosted her "Twentieth-Century" Ladies' Club meetings a few times a year.

Grandmother was seventy-five by the time I was ten, so she was beginning to slow down and entertained her friends much less. She was a simple, country woman who loved cooking and watching her favorite tv programs of the 1970s with me, like *The Carol Burnett Show*, *The Lawrence Welk Show*, and *The Ed Sullivan Show*. I remember Grandmother as a serious, quiet woman who was not warm or affectionate. However, once a year, I saw her get excited to watch the *Miss America* beauty pageant, which was always on a Saturday night in the spring. She'd invite me over to her house to eat a delicious dinner of spaghetti, salad, and pound cake. Then we would watch *Miss America* together. I thought the beauty pageants were dumb, but this was the only time of year that Grandmother came alive.

She'd say, "Well, back in '59, we had our own Miss Mississippi, Mary Ann Mobley, win the *Miss America* title. Elizabeth, when you are older, I want you to enter the Miss Mississippi pageant."

I protested and yelled, "No way, Grandmother. No beauty contests for me! I'm not going to Ole Miss or Mississippi State. I'm going to college far away, like in Virginia. Then, I'll have a career as an actress and live in a big, exciting city."

Grandmother would shake her head and say, "Good Lord, girl, you are something else."

Not only did I feel different from my family growing up, but I felt different from my friends, too. When my girlfriends wanted to play with baby dolls and pretend they were married with children, I would roll my eyes and say, "I don't want any stupid babies. I might not even get married. I'm gonna live in a big city and be on the stage. Don't you girls have any ambition?" Then I'd take out my Malibu Barbie and her townhouse with the wicker furniture. I'd pretend Barbie was a single career woman. My friends would stare at me in shock and disbelief.

As a teenager, I often felt sad and lonely, especially when my friends started to get crushes on boys. I felt different from my classmates, but I couldn't yet articulate how. When my friends started spending more time with their boyfriends than they spent with me, I felt jealous. Those fun "spend-the-night" parties, where we talked all night confessing our secret dreams, happened less often. My friends' dreams for the future were always about getting married and having children. I felt annoyed and bored when the conversation shifted to those topics.

Mama and I were close as mother and daughter, and we shared a spiritual connection. Twice a year while I was in elementary school, Mama and I would go on Methodist retreats on the Mississippi Gulf Coast in Biloxi. (We were Episcopalian, but the Methodists had better hymns and casseroles). The retreats were called CFOs–that's Camp Farthest Out! (What can I say, it was the seventies!) In the six-hour car ride on the way to the coast, Mama and I would sing "You Are My Sunshine" together, written by Jimmie Davis and Charles Mitchell,

> *You are my sunshine,*
> *My only sunshine.*
> *You make me happy,*
> *When skies are gray.*
> *You'll never know dear,*
> *How much I love you,*
> *Please don't take my sunshine away.*

Both Mama and Daddy grew up Southern Baptist, but in 1959, Mama decided she'd had enough of the Baptist Church. She said she was sick and tired of hearing the minister scold the women in the congregation as being "cocktail-sippin', cigarette smokin', good for nothin' housewives." Mama said she walked out in the middle of the minister's sermon. The next Sunday, she joined the tiny Episcopal church down the street. (This story became a family legend.)

Mama explained in her slow, Southern drawl, "I'd had it with that male chauvinist preacher. I walked out of that service, and it was the talk of the town! I intentionally joined the quietest, most elegant church in town, Grace Episcopal. It took your Daddy five more years before he joined. And your father's mother has never forgiven me for leaving First Baptist and joining Grace Episcopal Church."

I admired Mama for taking a stand. I wish she had done this more often.

Mama and Daddy were very social and enjoyed entertaining other couples. They belonged to a group called "The Supper Club." Every Saturday night, they would have dinner with five other couples. They took turns hosting in one another's homes. When they hosted it at our house, I remember hearing stories and howls of laughter. The next morning, the ornate silver ashtrays were filled with cigarette butts, and empty shot glasses were scattered across the counter. Apparently, in the 1950s and 60s, Chickasaw County was dry, so each couple in The Supper Club took a turn and drove to Memphis, a hundred and twenty miles north, and loaded their trunks with liquor–mostly scotch, bourbon, and vodka.

When I was eight or nine, The Supper Club ended abruptly. I'm not sure why. Maybe the drinking got out of hand. Some of the older couples started having grandchildren and traveling. They were getting older, and somehow their friendships faded.

About this time, Mama started getting more religious. She joined the charismatic movement - a trend of mainstream Christianity - which emphasized "spiritual gifts" such as speaking in tongues and prophecy. It was a far cry from the reserved, detached Episcopal services.

Mama took me to charismatic conferences. I thought they were weird and couldn't understand how this brand of Christianity appealed to her. Maybe it was the emotional component. Maybe it was the music. Was it the dramatic altar call? Mostly, I think Mama was drawn to this kind of religious expression to fill an emptiness inside her. She felt dissatisfied in her marriage. Daddy had become more depressed, detached, and overweight. Sadly, they had grown apart.

I remember once when Mama, Daddy, and I went to some rural church for a "speaking in tongues" testimonial at the Church of God of Prophecies. The minister got very loud and emotional. He seemed to be in some kind of trance and was speaking in a strange, unknown language. Mama explained that the Bible teaches in Corinthians that speaking in tongues is a spiritual gift that the Holy Spirit gives to believers. The language is unknown even to the speaker. Some people have the gift of interpretation, but at this service, whatever it was, it was strange. It sounded like a Middle Eastern language with short, chopped-up syllables. I remember looking at Daddy with a pleading look that must have been communicating I wanted out of there. It was scary. I felt surrounded by unpredictable strangers who were yelling out, "Praise the Lord!" They raised their hands, and some fell out in the aisles.

Daddy grabbed my hand. He whispered to me, "Come on, baby. We're gonna go walk around the block and take a break from this circus."

I was grateful Daddy rescued me from the fundamentalists.

At home, Mama grew more insistent that we have family devotional hours every night. We took turns reading from a book called More Little Visits with God. I remember the cover had a picture of an old man with a white beard, representing God, holding a little girl in his lap. That's a limited, patriarchal image of the Divine I've worked hard on to transform. Every morning, Mama read Bible verses from cards in a little plastic container.

Sometimes Daddy would groan and say, "Oh, Nita, can't we take a break from all these Bible verses?" He and I would give each other this look of understanding each other's frustrations. We'd roll our eyes and chuckle. Mama calmly replied, "It is my responsibility to provide a Christian home for us."

"Honey," he'd say to me. "She's just trying to be a good Christian Mama cuz she loves you so much."

On some level, I knew and felt that Mama loved me deeply. She took her role as a mother seriously and felt the responsibility to influence me as a Christian. Mama and Daddy were not perfect parents. They didn't have the benefit of psychotherapy or counseling. Long after they were gone, I realized the gifts they gave me–a foundation of love, a passion for community and connection, boarding school, college, and graduate school education, an interest in international travel, curiosity about other people, and a commitment to spiritual growth.

In the summer of 1967, when I was four years old, Mama and her older sisters bought a large Victorian summer house in the Cumberland mountains in Monteagle, Tennessee, that they called "Southern Comfort." The house was in a gated community called Monteagle Assembly, which dated back to 1882, when the Sunday School Convention of Tennessee created an educational congress for Sunday school teachers. (To this day, this community still has summer religious, cultural, and educational programs, as well as programs for children and youth.)

The house Mama, Aunt Liber, and Aunt Frannie bought was a large two-story Queen Anne-style house built in 1885. It was one of the first boarding houses built in Monteagle Assembly. In 1967, they bought it fully furnished for $5,000. They named the house "Southern Comfort" for their Southern sisterhood and for those lively porch parties they had where they wore their long Mumu dresses that looked like old draperies. Daddy and my uncles would occasionally visit for a long weekend, but for most of the summers of my childhood, it was Mama, Aunt Liber, Aunt Frannie, and me. (My siblings and cousins were between ten and twenty years older than I was, so for the first ten years of my life, they were away at college and summer jobs.) I had interesting friendships with girls my age who also vacationed in Monteagle. They were from exciting Southern cities like Atlanta, Memphis, and Nashville. Southern Comfort was always filled with a tribe of women and girls. We all had an unspoken understanding and respect for the power of story. How I loved hearing those porch stories. You see, in the South, porch time is sacred visiting time. Nobody's in a hurry.

My Aunt Liber and my Aunt Frannie were a huge part of my childhood. The oldest was Aunt Liber, the extroverted, serious-scotch-drinkin', cigarette-smokin' storyteller. I am her namesake. I loved the way she would say my name, especially on her second scotch. She sounded like a Southern Mae West, but classier.

"Elizabeth, my darlin' namesake, let's go sit on the porch and I'll tell you some stories about growin' up in the Mississippi Delta. I'll tell you stories your Mama doesn't even know."

My Aunt Frannie was the sweetest, most affectionate aunt, and the best cook. She's the one who got up early with me every morning to look for rocks, and I loved playing dress-up wearing her high heels, stomping up and down the stairs. I loved Aunt Frannie and can still hear her saying, "You darlin', precious, girl. Do you know how much I love you? Do you really know? I love you so much, my heart could melt."

She said these words to me every summer of my childhood, adolescence, and young adult years.

Mama, the youngest sister, was shy, very proper, and the most religious. She'd say, "It's time for me to read Scripture and then go to my prayer group. Don't forget, we have family devotion hour tonight."

Mama and I remained close even during my boarding school days. I attended an Episcopal boarding school in Vicksburg, Mississippi in the ninth grade. In the tenth grade, I transferred to St. Andrew's School, which was also an Episcopal boarding school in the beautiful Cumberland Mountains of central Tennessee, near "Southern Comfort" in Monteagle. My parents had encouraged my siblings and me to go to boarding schools to receive a better education than the local public school in Okolona could provide. As I mentioned before, Mama supported me in all kinds of ways. She attended every play, choral concert, and parents' weekends. Sometimes, Daddy came with her, but Mama was the one I could always count on. I was her baby, and she indulged me. But by the time I became a teenager, I was annoyed by how much she talked about Jesus and how she reminded me to stay a virgin until I married.

"Now I know the Lord will choose the right man for you to marry. And you know you must save yourself for him."

Needless to say, as you know, I disagreed with her on both counts.

On the porch at Southern Comfort, Mama sat in her yellow rocking chair under the hum of the ceiling fan. She leaned into her sister Liber and said, "Sistah, what ever happened to those wonderful love letters Mother wrote Daddy during World War I, when she was at the University of Chicago?"

Aunt Liber took a drag from her cigarette with her ruby-red, Revlon lips.

"Oh, baby girl, those lettahs! Weren't they beautifully written? Mothah was so cultured and literary. You know she taught the writer Eudora Welty in high school in Jackson."

I would chime in. Even as a ten-year-old girl, I knew the value of family history and family keepsakes.

"Are they in your house, Aunt Liber? Where are they? I would love to read them!"

"Oh, where are those letters? Well, they are probably in a safe place somewhere in my house down on Macon Plantation. I'll find 'em, and next summer, we'll read them together!"

Sadly, Aunt Liber never found them. When I visited her with

Mama at her house in the Delta, after everyone went to bed, I'd sneak around, opening drawers and closets hoping to find those love letters. I didn't find them. But you know what? Everett, my cousin, found our grandparents' love letters. You know where? Under Aunt Liber's bed, where they had been for over forty years! Now, she hadn't slept in her bed for many years thanks to a bit of a hoarding problem she had that made the bed unavailable. Aunt Liber had slept on the couch for decades. Everett scanned all our grandparents' love letters into the computer to share with the rest of us. They wrote passionate love letters to one another in their younger days of courting.

To give you some understanding of my grandparents in the early 1900s, here's a bit about who they were as young people.

My maternal grandmother was Marguerite Chadwick Park. Her grandchildren called her "Bopie." Having grown up in Jackson, she was unusually educated for her generation of women. She actually did graduate work in 1917 and 1918 at the University of Chicago, where she studied education, American history, and the poetry of Tennyson and Wordsworth.

My grandfather was Forrest Graham Cooper from Forrest, Mississippi. We called him "Pop." He was an attorney, and a pilot in the Air Force in World War I. Bopie and Pop had a long-distance romance for a year and a half during the war. While she was in Chicago studying, he was teaching young pilots to fly, stationed at various Air Force bases all over the country. He was hoping to be sent to France, but never was. They wrote each other passionate love letters nearly every day. Thanks to cousin Everett, who found these precious letters, I have copies of 193 of them. Here are some of my favorite ones. My grandmother wrote to her beloved:

July 2, 1917
Chicago

My brave, happy adorable, big-hearted laddie,

Oh, lover boy, I simply must see you! I think of you so constantly that my program here is interrupted. This is no way for an ex-teacher, medical secretary, war relief worker, sedate woman past a quarter of a century to act! Lover boy, my capacity for your dailies (daily letters) is positively anaconder-ish, boa constrictor-ish. The pigeon-holes in my brain which register and receive them are cavernous, mammoth, cavish. Is that strong enough to make you understand how much I want them? And if I want the letters that way, can you stretch your imagination to conceive how much more I want the author of those letters?

You Mr. Aviator, you of the astounding mid-air stunts, could not even make a descent beginning to the flight I have in mind.

Tell me sweetheart, would you rather be my lover or my husband?

I am loving you now and always,

Your wife to be,
Marguerite

And then, he responded to her.

My only girl,

Today, I would be delighted to take you in my arms and crush you, and say soft things. I am certainly aware of the limitations of my mere man heart, but I do love you mightily.

Keep that sacred fountain pen of yours. Keep it for memory's sake. For it has unfolded to me the sweetest story outside the Bible and a mother's love. We shall marry soon.

All my love,
Your devoted man boy,
Forrest

Who writes letters like that anymore? Who even writes letters at all? Can you imagine how forward and sexy my grandmother's letters were? What a passionate wordsmith she was! I love the combination of her clever, elegant vocabulary mixed with her provocative bawdiness. What a tease Bopie was! I had no idea about this part of her; I only knew her as a paralyzed woman living in the nursing home for five years, recovering from her stroke. But in her youth, Bopie was a bold, independent, educated woman. She did not follow her culture's expectations. Most women of her generation at age twenty-five were back home in Mississippi, 800 miles away–married, having babies, and cooking three big meals a day in their antebellum kitchens. My grandmother, Marguerite, had a courageous spirit. And I know I have a part of her in me. I, too, have taken a bit of a different path. I have not followed my culture's expectations either.

I've been reflecting on my complicated relationship with the Southern culture that shaped me. There are some things I adore and abhor about my homeland. It's easy to fall in love with the South immediately because the people are so friendly. Small Southern towns offer hospitality, good food, and a close-knit community of loyal friends. Southern accents are comforting, with a soothing rhythm to them. In his novel, *Mississippi Sissy*, writer, Kevin Sessums describes recalling his Mississippi homeland and hearing the "rich sounds of the voices that surrounded me and from those sounds come the words ... the movement of conversation!" I feel a sense of connection with other Southerners when I hear those softer accents. We enjoy a slower pace of life, allowing us to appreciate some of the simpler things in life, like how the sound of cicadas and crickets on a warm summer night creates a sensual and romantic atmosphere. Spring arrives early in the South, and is full of intoxicating colors and scents like magenta azaleas, fragrant, bright yellow daffodils, and lavender butterfly bushes.

People who've lived in the South their whole lives are steeped in story and community. The South has produced many talented writers such as Eudora Welty, Flannery O'Connor, Alice Walker, Maya Angelou, Dorothy Allison, William Faulkner, Willie Morris, and Pat Conroy. Unlike in more hurried parts of the world, we Southerners will take the time to tell our stories and listen to others' stories. We value knowing people and being known. Blues music started in the South, in Mississippi, from African Americans with roots in spirituals, and African American work songs. In the South, we are fascinated with our eccentric family members and friends. William Faulkner said the difference between the North and the South is that "in the North, crazy relatives are hidden in the attic. In the South, we put them on the front porch and let them wave to everybody."

As I mentioned before, I love that Southern church women have a refined talent for throwing a damn good party after a funeral. It's full of those delicious casseroles, fried chicken, pot roast, sinful desserts, plenty of booze (unless it was a Baptist funeral), and storytelling that continues late into the night.

There are clearly things I wish I could change about the South. There is still so much inherent racism and segregation. (My hometown elementary school only integrated in 1970. The Ku Klux Klan was active there in the 1980s and 90s.) The majority of the Deep South is filled with conservative, right-wing Christians, who have a rigid attachment to a narrow "faith-based" and fear-based mindset. Unsurprisingly, the Republican Party rules with lots of sexist older white men. More surprisingly, their women defend them. In lockstep with this mindset, there is plenty of homophobia and heterosexism in the South, and stubborn resistance to change. Maybe because of that deep storytelling tradition, gossip flies fast in the South, and you can still find a lack of trust and remaining resentment towards Northern people. For example, people from north of the Mason-Dixon line are still called "Yankees" from the "War of Northern Aggression."

Despite these limitations and the shadow side of the Deep South, I still feel a strong connection to it–especially for my home state, Mississippi. Generations of my ancestors lived long lives in those small towns where family, faith, and community mattered. Mississippi gave me strong roots and an appreciation for stories told on porches, at funerals, weddings, and even in the check-out line at the Piggly Wiggly.

CHAPTER 4

Memphis Cotton Carnival Catastrophe

M y teen years were filled with an unhappiness and a sense of frustration that I didn't yet understand. When I was sixteen, my parents mentioned the possibility of giving me a debutante ball. This is a Southern tradition that originated during the nineteenth century when upper-class European families presented their marriageable daughters at these formal events. The word "debutante" means "female beginner." These debutante balls were also called "coming-out parties." (Little did I know that fifteen years down the road, my future held a much livelier kind of coming out party.) Alas, my focus at sixteen was not on debutante balls, but school.

As I mentioned before, I attended two different Episcopal boarding schools during my high school years to prepare for college. In the ninth grade, I was unhappy at my school in Vicksburg, Mississippi. The students there partied a lot and came from cities like New Orleans, Memphis, and Little Rock. As a straight-laced, straight-A student, I was a misfit at that school. I loved the beauty of the colonial architecture and the rolling hills of Vicksburg, but I was miserable otherwise. I remember liking my Spanish teacher, Ms. Del Gato, my English teacher, Mrs. Stone, and an encouraging P.E. teacher, Ms. Dot Fitzgerald, who taught me how to water ski. But I wanted to go to a boarding school that had a theater department and a chorus. So, in the tenth grade, I was happy to transfer to St. Andrew's School, an Episcopal boarding school in the beautiful Cumberland Mountains of Tennessee, near the tiny liberal arts college town of Sewanee, seven miles from our summer home, Southern Comfort.

I excelled at St. Andrew's academically. The classes were more interesting and challenging than the ones at All Saints'. I was aware most of my female friends had crushes on the boys. Although I thought a few guys in my Southern literature class and my theatre class were cute, I never had a boyfriend there. It bothered me a little because my closest friends all had boyfriends by their senior year. At that point, I definitely felt different and lonely, but I told myself I was there to get a good education to prepare me for college. Boyfriends were not a part of my academic life.

In the mid-1980s, I attended Randolph-Macon Woman's College in Lynchburg, Virginia, which was a woman's college at that time. Academically, R-MWC was a good liberal arts college. I felt I was in a constant struggle trying to fit in with girls who enjoyed those awful fraternity parties at men's liberal arts colleges, like Washington and Lee University and Hampden-Sydney College. How could they put up with guys who were drunk and obviously disrespectful toward young women? These were not the men I wanted to date.

My parents were concerned that I didn't have a boyfriend. Daddy encouraged me to follow in my older sister's footsteps and attend the

Memphis Cotton Carnival, which is now called Carnival Memphis. This was an elitist festival founded in 1931 to help the city of Memphis raise money for the cotton industry so that Memphis could keep up with other Southern cities. It grew into a huge celebration with a king, queen, and royal court of cotton that involved people from all over the Mid-South. It was like the New Orleans Mardi Gras on a smaller scale. The "Royal Court" was made up of young women who were mostly freshmen and sophomores in college. The Queen was a lady a couple of years older, and the King was a prominent business leader.

I wasn't crazy about joining this upper crust, patriarchal tradition of the Memphis Cotton Carnival. I didn't think there would be many college students from Virginia. Most of the students who participated in these sorts of things went to Ole' Miss, Vanderbilt University, and Southwestern College, now called Rhodes College.

In spite of my resistance, Daddy kept pushing me to apply for the carnival.

"Baby girl, you'll meet some fine Southern gentlemen from the wealthiest families in the Mid-South. You surely are not meeting fellas up at that girl's college in Virginia, where the women libbers and lesbians go."

"Daddy, I go to a women's college, not a girls' school. And there's nothing wrong with feminists or lesbians."

Daddy would frown and shake his head at me.

Mama was kind of on the fence about me attending the Memphis Cotton Carnival.

"Well, honey, your sister enjoyed it," Mama said, "but she had her boyfriend, Sam, to escort her. I'm thrilled they married two years later. Since you don't have a boyfriend, it might be hard. But I think the organizers can set you up with some nice Memphis boys to escort you to the balls."

So, I gave in to Daddy's dream. I applied to the Memphis Cotton Carnival. I had to write a resume and get older ladies in my hometown to write me letters of recommendation. It was a big deal, and not in a good way, but in a pain-in-the-ass way. I was selected to represent my town as "Lady of the Realm" in the Royal Court of Cotton. Daddy was thrilled.

I had to get fitted for the cotton dresses we were supposed to wear. I remember the long dress was red and white floral with red spaghetti straps. The other two dresses were shorter ones that were pink and yellow, respectively. We had to wear white wedge sandals, with horrible pantyhose in horrendously humid June. I hated sweating like a pig.

Daddy said, "Hallelujah! I'm so glad you'll be in those country clubs in that Memphis Cotton Carnival! Your Mama and I are so proud of you!"

Mama said, "Glory be, Elizabeth! Remember that Jesus is gonna choose the perfect man for you to marry. Maybe your future husband will be in that Royal Court of Cotton! You'll get married and have babies. That's what Southern ladies do!"

I spouted off to her and said, "Marriage and babies are not for me. I don't want to be in the Junior League or the Garden Club."

I tried to make the best of the situation. I was assigned a roommate, a gal named Helen from Indianola, a Delta town, which was also Mama's hometown. Helen and I talked on the phone the month before the carnival. She attended Hollins College, a woman's college located in Roanoke, Virginia, an hour from my college. But she had a boyfriend, which meant she had an escort to those damn balls at the country clubs. And she was transferring to Ole Miss to be closer to home.

Helen and I were assigned to stay at the Dobbs' family home. Mr. Dobbs was third generation owner of one of the largest car dealerships in Memphis. They lived in a huge mansion with a tennis court and a pool. They had an African American maid who dressed in a white uniform and brought us breakfast in bed. This made me feel so uncomfortable. I never relished my role as a privileged white girl.

I was miserable that week. I had been assigned a blind date to escort me on the first two nights of parties at the country clubs. His name was Sheldon Beauregard. For readers who are not Southern, you might be thinking I got creative and made up his name. I promise you this is true. He had written to me on stationery that had "Sons of the Confederacy" in navy letters at the top. At this point, you may think this sounds like a David Sedaris story. It turns out, Sheldon was an alcoholic dropout from Vanderbilt University. He finally showed up, drunk as a skunk and terribly late, on the third night of the carnival. I was disgusted with him and told him off.

"Sheldon, you're drunk and two hours late. And thanks to you, I was the only girl who had no escort to those huge country clubs. I slowly did the walk of shame at the back of the line."

I tried to fit in with the other girls I met at the Cotton Carnival. There was this one sorority girl who drove me nuts. She had long blonde hair, huge boobs, a tiny waist, and an annoying Tennessee twang.

On the first day, she looked me over from head to toe and said, "Hey, I'm Lou Anne. I'm a Chi O at Ole Miss majoring in elementary education. This is my boyfriend, Jimmy Bob. Where do you go to school? Where's your boyfriend? What sorority are you in?"

I took a deep breath and replied,

"I'm Elizabeth. I go to Randolph-Macon Woman's College in Virginia, where we read a lot. I'm an English major. We don't have sororities. And I don't have a boyfriend."

Lou Anne frowned and placed her hands on her hips.

"Oh… no boyfriend? No sorority? English major at a girls' school? You're one of those bookish girls. Well, do you like boys at all? You're not even drunk! Honey, are you sure you're Southern?"

I rolled my eyes and walked away. Her questions drove me to drink too many gin and tonics that night. I knew I would never be able to fit in. This was not my tribe. In one way, I felt like a failure, but I knew this sexist, elitist culture didn't fit with my values. I was relieved when that cotton carnival was over. I knew I was saying good-bye to the traditions of the Deep South. Even at twenty, I knew there was more to life than gowns, crowns, and small Southern towns.

CHAPTER 5

Coming Out Personally and Professionally

After I graduated from college, I moved to the Washington, DC area. I had various jobs as an elementary school teacher, and as a tour guide at The Woodrow Wilson House before I attended graduate school at The George Washington University to get a master's degree in counseling. I dated many guys throughout my twenties, but none of those relationships felt right to me. Fast forward to my life in 1994. I was finally comfortable enough with my newly tried-on lesbian identity to join a coming out support group for lesbians at The Whitman-Walker Clinic for gays and lesbians in DC. I remember that first group session. It was a Monday evening in September. I remember wearing my 1993 Lesbian and Gay March on Washington t-shirt and khaki shorts with purple sandals. I walked into a room of ten very butch and androgynous-looking lesbians, except for one woman who wore makeup like me. I remember the feminist activist dyke wearing a flannel shirt and cargo pants; the conservative-looking, closeted Lutheran minister in her khakis, men's belt, and a pink button-down oxford shirt; and the preppy femme with heavy makeup who wore pearls, a white blouse, a navy blazer and skirt, and black flats.

I was the only one in the group who said I had struggled with deciding whether I was bisexual or lesbian. Everyone else said they'd felt different from other girls growing up. Most of them described themselves as "tomboys" or athletic. I got a little bit of push back from some of the women for even considering the bisexual identity.

One woman, Lara, asked, "But for the long haul in your life, do you see yourself with a man or a woman? I mean, don't you want to choose at some point?"

I replied, "Oh, I guess, but right now, I'm not focused on the rest of my life."

As you know, I eventually decided that I was more lesbian than bisexual. I developed close friendships with two women around my age, Annie and Moe. We went out to dinner and then out dancing at bars in DC like The Phase 1, the oldest lesbian bar in the country, and Tracks, a huge warehouse where lots of gay men, lesbians, and "sexually curious types" went dancing. It was the 90s which meant great music. While moving to Whitney Houston, Michael Jackson, Melissa Ethridge, and Cher, I felt thrilled to belong to my lesbian and gay family.

I came out in my personal life in 1994, when I was thirty-one. That was also the year I got licensed in Virginia as a professional counselor at the women's counseling center, where I had volunteered, completed my internship, and then was hired as a counselor. My focus had initially been in career counseling, but once I started a graduate counseling program at The George Washington University, I became fascinated with feminist psychology, women's studies, and family systems theories.

I became acquainted with many smart women who were in graduate school and completing their internships. Most of them were older, married, straight women with kids, and several single, straight women. There were a few gay guys in my counseling program, but no lesbians.

There were only two other out lesbian therapists working at this women's center. I invited one of them to lunch to ask her about her coming out process. This woman returned my call and left me a voicemail message telling me she was very introverted, very busy, very private, and not very out. I was getting discouraged and feeling like I was the only lesbian.

All the counselors used an appointment book back in those pre-online days, highlighting their specialty areas and availabilities. I remember the first day I wrote "Lesbian and Gay Issues." It was the day I outed myself. I felt a combination of pride and anxiety but was pleased when some therapists began telling me about their lesbian nieces and gay nephews.

One day after a fascinating group supervision session with a psychologist leading us as counseling interns, I had a mind-blowing conversation with one of my colleagues, Sally. She was a few years older than me, very pretty and petite, with short, layered, golden-brown hair. I remember that we were both wearing purple dresses, pantyhose, and black, flat shoes. The year was 1995. I didn't know Sally very well, but I always appreciated her comments in the group about feminist psychology. She was getting her Ph.D. in psychology. We lingered in the room, chatting after everyone else had left. I was drawn to Sally and wanted to befriend her. I asked her how she liked her internship.

To my surprise, she said, "Well, I feel like a fish out of water here. Except for you, all the women counselors and interns are conservative, older, married women. I'm a lesbian and I'm guessing I'm the only one."

We were standing in between the door and a stained white, cheap-looking couch from Ikea. I literally fell over onto the couch,

"Holy shit, Sally! I never would have guessed! I started dating one of the volunteers here. I guess I'm a lesbian. This has surprised me. I've always dated men."

Sally's face beamed.

"Oh, girl! Thank God. I have a sister here! We should go to lunch and share our stories. I'll tell you all about DC lesbian culture."

Later that week, Sally and I met for a three-hour lunch on her day off. She looked different, wearing faded jeans, a sweatshirt, and black cowboy boots. She was driving a red Ford pickup truck. I thought this was odd–almost like she had a different look and identity in her personal life as a lesbian. I naively wondered if all lesbians wore cowboy boots and drove trucks. I must say though, I thought she was sexy as hell.

I discovered that Sally had a younger girlfriend. They'd been together for several years and shared a basement apartment in a suburb of DC. Sally and I talked for hours and connected deeply about feminist psychology and spirituality. She was the first real lesbian friend I had. We developed a sweet friendship, talking on the phone several times a week, and having long lunches. Sally took me to my first lesbian dance at a lesbian conference called "Passages" at The George Washington University. Eventually, she broke up with her girlfriend. I was definitely attracted to her, especially the nights we hung out in her new apartment and laughed, drank wine, and shared stories. Sally was also a talented artist and painted portraits of women. She once asked if she could sketch me (clothed, of course). It was awkward when she told me I had beautiful curvy hips.

"Well, Elizabeth, there's nothing like loving a woman, even though it's hard living in such a patriarchal, heterosexist, and homophobic culture," she told me.

One day, I received a call from Sally. She told me that she had attempted suicide and was in a treatment program at a psychiatric hospital, being treated for post-traumatic stress disorder and substance abuse. I was stunned. She'd never revealed these problems in the past six months of our friendship. Sally had seemed like a self-confident woman to me. After talking to my therapist and doing research, I discovered that it was common for gay and lesbian people to experience depression, anxiety, substance abuse, and to have suicidal ideation. This saddened me deeply. Unfortunately, our connection faded out. I have thought about her over the years and regretted that we didn't stay in touch.

Eventually, I came out in a larger way as a therapist. I joined a professional networking group for lesbian health professionals called the Lesbian Health and Wellness Network. We met every month and had interesting discussions on topics such as lesbian–competent psychotherapy, lesbian–competent medical services, and coming out professionally.

Such open dialogue led me to develop and facilitate workshops on lesbian dating and sexuality. I read every book on these topics I could find. Sometimes, I could "fake it 'til I made it." My newly found curiosity and passion for all things lesbian emboldened me. I also volunteered as a co-facilitator for a coming-out group for lesbians at the Whitman–Walker Clinic. My self-esteem blossomed.

Gradually, I got to know older lesbian therapists as well as social workers at the Whitman–Walker Clinic with whom I networked. I received training in Imago relationship therapy and began to see lesbian couples. I especially enjoyed leading a six-week support group for several young lesbian couples. I am grateful for the opportunities I've had to support many lesbians (and a few gay men) as a therapist. It has been an honor to help lesbians come out and live out with pride so they can live authentically.

My personal life, however, was more challenging. I was not happy with my short-lived, unsuccessful lesbian relationships. I dated several alcoholics, as well as some workaholics. I didn't see this in the beginning because the intense physical attraction I felt blinded me. I was having my lesbian adolescence. After each breakup, I felt lost and abandoned. The irony is somehow I continued my career as a psychotherapist and helped many lesbians and gay men come out and have healthier relationships. I remember often feeling like an imposter. I told myself, "God, if they only knew how fucked up my life was!" On the other hand, I think my family estrangement and wounding gave me an extra dose of compassion for my clients.

Although it was challenging coming out to my family, I'm grateful that I didn't have serious mental health problems such as clinical depression or substance abuse. I'm grateful for all of my coming out experiences. I have been with my spouse for nineteen years and married for eleven years. I'll tell you the story of how we met a little later.

In the past several years, I've come out to close to a thousand people performing my one-woman play, *A Lesbian Belle Tells....* Saying the title requires me to come out. Lesbians and queer women relate to my stories of coming out, lesbian culture, and family estrangement. Most of the time, straight people respond with interest and positivity. Occasionally, I get some stern looks or looks of surprise. I usually smile and move on.

At the beginning stages of writing this book, I was at a writing workshop in Pennsylvania. There were a few older conservative Christians at a lunch table. I started to dread saying the topic of the book I was writing, which you are now reading. I feared being judged. It required me to take a risk and be vulnerable. I could feel my heart race, and I began to sweat. So, I began to breathe deeply and give myself a pep talk. I gently told myself that I did not need these peoples' approval. I permitted myself to leave the table if it felt negative or unsafe. And I used humor, as I boldly said,

"My book is a memoir based on my one-woman play, *A Lesbian Belle Tells...*" (I said the title slowly, with confidence, and paused to let it register). Then I continued, "The stories in my play are my true experiences of growing up in Mississippi, coming out in DC, experiencing family estrangement, and finding love and belonging. It is a show with comedy and triumph over tragedy as only a lesbian belle can tell!"

I smiled and winked in my most Southern lipstick lesbian persona.

Everyone at the table laughed, and people asked me all kinds of questions. With twenty-five years of experience coming out (as we know, it's an ongoing process), I've become much more adept and confident when answering those questions.

CHAPTER 6

Mama Drama and Other Family Coming Out Moments

Although it was a risk for me to come out to my family, I was determined to live my life with integrity. The year I was closeted was stressful. I didn't enjoy feeling that I was carrying a secret. My secrecy caused me to feel ashamed of who I was, which I knew wasn't healthy. The necessity of watching everything I said about my personal life, so I didn't reveal information about the lesbian part of my life, was exhausting. I was limiting my conversations and my relationships with people I loved. I began to feel bad about myself for keeping a secret about my sexuality. When my new girlfriend, Kat and I moved in together, I knew it was time to come out to my mother. I didn't know how to tell her this story, the story of the first woman I truly loved.

I met Kat when I was thirty-one, at that same progressive Episcopal church, St. Mark's, where I'd had my last boyfriend. Kat was six years younger than I–a shapely tomboy-looking kind of gal with short curly blonde hair and blue eyes. She was the youth director at St. Mark's, and everyone loved her. She was smart, engaging, and great with teenagers. She and I became friends at a women's spirituality retreat. Kat and I were both exploring DC lesbian culture together.

I remember the moment I realized I was attracted to her. It was when I saw her sitting at her church office desk in a long, flowing, hippy skirt. I noticed her rainbow anklet and how sexy her ankles looked. I felt a wave of desire shoot through my body. Then I pushed it away. I told myself it was safer just to be friends.

On a cold, rainy Friday night that January, Kat and I were sitting at a Capitol Hill bar called The Hawk N Dove. I was raving about how special our friendship was. I felt safe and inspired by her and shared this with her. We shared our journeys in therapy together, as well as discussing books on feminist Christian theology and Buddhism. We read poetry by Mary Oliver and E. E. Cummings to each other. When I told Kat how much our friendship meant to me, she proclaimed, "I think this is much more than friendship. I think you're hot and we should date!"

And so began our passionate romance. No matter what your sexual orientation is, I bet you can remember the emotional and sexual high you'd feel for days with a new love. Sleep matters little. It didn't take long before I realized this relationship with Kat felt right. I knew I was in love with Kat. After only four months of dating, we moved in together even though I was aware Kat had plans to attend Harvard Divinity School in four months.

Kat and I had been living together for about six weeks before my mother called with important news. I hadn't come out to my family yet. I was terrified of what my conservative Christian (Baptist-born, later to become a "frozen chosen" Episcopalian) mother would think. I already knew Daddy was obsessed with the idea of me marrying a rich Southern gentleman. I was guessing they would be horrified and very homophobic. Little did I know how painful and dramatic my coming out process would be.

It was a June morning when Mama called to tell me my beloved great Aunt Malva died in Columbia, Maryland, where she lived with her husband. This news deeply saddened me since I had developed a friendship with Malva and her husband, Red. They fascinated me with their civil rights activism in the 1960s, which forced them to flee from Mississippi. A well-known journalist, Hodding Carter, wrote a book about their story in 1965 called *So the Heffners Left McComb*. This was the only part of my Mississippi family of my parents' generation that was politically and socially liberal. I had spent many hours at their home in the last couple of years hearing their stories.

Mama told me she was going to the funeral and would be staying with me for several days. I panicked. I hadn't mentioned I now had a "roommate." I didn't have the courage to come out to Mama or anyone in my family. So, I took a deep breath and told Mama a partial truth–that since I had a roommate in a small apartment, she would have to stay in a hotel.

"Hotel!" she yelled. "But I always stay with you! Roommate! You never mentioned you had a roommate. You've been living alone for over two years. Is your roommate that tomboyish girl I met at your birthday party? Are you living with that Kat who wears those ugly, mannish shoes?"

Terrified, I decided to tell the truth. "Yeah, Mama. Kat's my… my best friend."

"Well, I think she's a lesbian! You better be careful, cuz she might try to turn you into one!"

I then took a deep breath and began to tell the truth about my sexuality that would turn my life upside down for many years to come.

"Mama, she's not turning me into a lesbian. I am a lesbian! And I'm in love with Kat!"

My mild-mannered, Mississippi Mama totally flipped out and raged at me, screaming, "No! No! This can't be! You were not born that way. This is a terrible, rebellious choice you are making. This is not who you are, young lady! You're angry at men. The homosexual lifestyle is unnatural and sinful!"

I yelled back, "Mama, this who I am. There's nothing wrong with me. And it doesn't matter whether I was born a lesbian or if I choose to be a lesbian. The truth is, I am in love with Kat!"

Mama continued with her judgmental, outrageous reaction.

"Don't ever speak of her or your perverted lifestyle. Don't come home to visit your father and me. And don't you dare tell anyone else in the family!"

"Well, I already told Aunt Malva, Uncle Red, and all my other aunts and some cousins, too! I'm not hiding in the closet. It's my life, and I'll do as I please!"

"Elizabeth Frances McCain, you disgust me!"

She hung up on me and canceled her trip for Aunt Malva's funeral. I went to her funeral and came out to several other cousins. All those relatives supported me. After several glasses of Chardonnay, my cousin, Carla, Aunt Malva's daughter, called my mother and told her it was a shame that she didn't come to Malva's funeral. And Carla told my mother she should accept me for who I was.

Mama hung up on her, too.

Unfortunately, two months later, my girlfriend, Kat, moved to Cambridge, Massachusetts, and broke my heart when she suddenly ended our relationship. I was shocked and became depressed. I didn't see it coming. I thought she was my soulmate. We had talked about having a future together. I even had planned to move to Boston to live with her in a year. I felt so abandoned. It took me at least two years to grieve that breakup.

Mama wouldn't see me or talk to me for a year and a half. I received manipulative, judgmental letters begging me to turn away from my "sinful life." She even mailed me some pitiful book written by a Christian psychiatrist, insisting that homosexuality was a mental illness that could be cured with "conversion therapy." I burned the book in a releasing ritual with my new lesbian friends witnessing in their backyard.

For the next several years, I did a lot of psychotherapy with a lesbian therapist. I also saw a feminist lesbian spiritual director and attended a support group on sexuality and spirituality for lesbians.

I got a tremendous amount of support from my therapist, my St. Mark's choir community, and my new lesbian friends in my coming-out group. But nothing anyone said or did erased my feelings of abandonment, rage, resentment, and deep grief.

As I mentioned before, I dated some difficult women who were emotionally unavailable. I was an emotional wreck from my family estrangement. To be fair, I'm certain that my grief, anger, and despair were difficult for the women I dated. My relationships never made it past ten months. I didn't feel like I fit into the lesbian community. I rarely met women who looked as feminine as I was. Nor did I know many Southern lesbians who had the courage to come out to their families. Clearly, I was repeating old family-of-origin themes of abandonment and not fitting into a defined culture.

I occasionally mailed PFLAG literature and books on coming out to Mama. I had told her I wasn't ready to come out to Daddy. Mama finally broke down and told Daddy.

His response was, "Don't ever come home again! You're out of this family, and out of the will. Nobody wants to be around you. I think you should move to another country."

I was devastated and stunned by Daddy's hostile homophobia. I spent holidays with friends. I got tired of people telling me that eventually, they thought my family would come around and accept me. I knew they wouldn't.

My siblings also judged and rejected me. Remember, they were much older than me. My oldest brother, Jem, seventeen years my senior, had been a rebellious hippy at Ole Miss in the 1960s. (He was called "Mad Dog McCain" in his fraternity). When I came out to him, I had hoped he would be accepting. I didn't realize he had become a fundamentalist Christian in the meantime.

His response to me was, "The Bible says that homosexuality is an abomination. I think you are practicing witchcraft in the woods with radical lesbians. And they are brainwashing you."

Practicing witchcraft in the woods with radical lesbians wasn't far from the truth since I had explored lesbian Pagan circles. But being accused of being brainwashed was ridiculous.

I was furious at Jem and set firm boundaries with him to stop judging me.

I then came out to my other brother, Reynolds, who is twelve years older than me and a conservative neurologist. His response was, "Elizabeth, homosexuality is a mental illness!"

I told him he was wrong. Didn't he know that the diagnostic manual of mental disorders had admitted they were wrong in listing homosexuality as a mental illness? In 1973, the American Psychiatric Association removed the diagnosis of homosexuality from the second edition of the Diagnostic and Statistical Manual.

And when I came out to my sister Marguerite, a buttoned-up, serious attorney almost ten years my senior, her response was, "This choice of yours will be destructive to our family. I don't think this is who you are."

When I told her I was happy, she said, "Elizabeth, life is not about being happy."

Not only was I disappointed that none of my siblings were supporting me, but I was also sad to realize they didn't value happiness and authenticity.

Luckily, I had a loving cast of colorful aunts who softened the blow of the rejection from my parents and siblings. Growing up, Aunt Frannie, one of Mama's older sisters, was my sweetest and most affectionate aunt. My earliest memory of her was looking deeply into my eyes when I was around four and saying,

"Darlin, do you know how much your Aunt Frannie loves you? You precious girl, I love you so much my heart could burst!"

Then, she would put her arms around me and kiss my forehead.

Aunt Frannie also loved to pat me on my back. She also patted Mama and their older sister, my Aunt Liber. It was her way of physically reminding everyone of her presence and love. It was comforting growing up feeling the depth of Aunt Frannie's love for everyone.

Mama and Aunt Liber kind of felt sorry for Aunt Frannie because they said she married a "Yankee" man from Akron, OH. Apparently, she had been engaged to two men before that (not at the same time) who were both tragically killed in World War II.

Aunt Liber would say, "Bless Frannie's sweet little heart. She's missed living in the South. She's had to work so hard in that cold Akron, Ohio–teaching little Yankee school children."

Mama would say, "Yeah, honey. I know. We are so lucky we didn't have to work. I'm glad the three of us can be together every summer here at Southern Comfort."

Years later, I decided Aunt Frannie would be the easiest aunt to whom I could come out. She didn't wear her Christianity on her sleeve like Aunt Liber and Mama did. And I never heard Aunt Frannie say a judgmental thing about anyone.

A few weeks after the disastrous phone call in which I came out to Mama, I decided to come out to Aunt Frannie. On a humid June afternoon, I called her.

"Hey, Aunt Frannie!!"

"Elizabeth, you darlin! How are you, Precious?"

"I'm okay, but I'm having a hard time with Mama."

There was a long pause.

"Aunt Frannie, I'm a lesbian. I'm in love with a woman. I told Mama on the phone before she came to visit me to go to Aunt Malva's funeral. She freaked out and told me I'm a sinner and that it's wrong. She screamed and cried and said I couldn't go home to visit, nor could I come to Monteagle this summer."

"Oh, Honey. I'm so sorry. Well, your Mama is very religious. And I guess she was hoping you'd marry and have children. But I'll tell you, sweet girl, I'm not surprised at all."

"Really, Aunt Frannie? What do you mean?"

"Well, it crossed my mind that you might be gay, or at least considering it. You've never been with a man for very long. I remember that one boyfriend you had in college. I knew you weren't in love with him. And I knew you were a feminist and went to a woman's college. It makes sense, honey."

"Can you talk to Mama, Aunt Frannie?"

"Well, darlin, I don't think I'll change your Mama's mind. I'll tell her I think this is who you are, and that she can't change that."

"Thank you, Aunt Frannie. Mama is such a stubborn Aries. And she's gone overboard on Jesus! But I wanted you to know the truth, Aunt Frannie. I'm sure Mama won't mention this to you at all. She's ashamed of having a lesbian daughter."

"I'll let her know you called me and told me. I'm so sorry, honey. I'll keep both of y'all in my thoughts and prayers."

"All right, Aunt Frannie. Thank you."

"You're welcome, precious girl. You know how much I love you, right?"

"Yes, Aunt Frannie! You love me so much your heart could burst, right?"

"Absolutely, sweet girl!"

Aunt Sue was my most glamorous aunt. She had big hair, big diamonds, and drove a big Cadillac. As Daddy's younger sister, Aunt Sue grew up in my hometown and left Mississippi in 1950 when she married and moved to Houston, Texas, where her husband, my Uncle Bill, got a job as an engineer.

Aunt Sue was also my most attentive aunt. She always remembered my birthday by sending a nice gift and calling me. The gifts were always beautifully wrapped in fancy boxes from Neiman Marcus or Lord + Taylor. She got me girly gifts like colorful purses, scarves, and sweaters. Every summer she came to visit her mother, my grandmother, who lived around the corner from us. I loved hearing her stories of what a quaint town Okolona was "back in the day." She talked about dances she and her classmates had out at the city park in the "pavilion" where I took tap, ballet, and jazz dance classes in the 1970s. I loved knowing the history of those old buildings and imagining my Aunt Sue dressed in glamorous evening gowns in the 1940s.

One day when I was around thirty-two, Aunt Sue called me. We hadn't talked in over a year. I had been out for a couple of years at that point but avoided returning her calls. I knew Aunt Sue was very Baptist, and since my parents had rejected me so harshly, I feared facing her judgment of me.

Aunt Sue got right to the point of her call. "Elizabeth, sweetie, I've met the nicest man, Andrew, here in Houston. He was visiting his father. He lives near you in Alexandria, Virginia. He was on President Bush's staff. He's refined, young, and has quite a portfolio! I hope you don't mind, dear, that I gave him your number. You're still single, right?"

I panicked. I knew that to be authentic, I had to come out to her.

"Well, Aunt Sue, I'm not single. I'm dating someone."

"Oh, you are? Well, your daddy hasn't mentioned that, and we talk every Sunday night."

"Well, he wouldn't tell you this, Aunt Sue. He's very upset at me."

"Oh, so he doesn't approve of your boyfriend? Honey, are you dating an older man?"

"No, ma'am."

"A younger man?"

"No, ma'am."

"A divorced man?"

"No, ma'am."

"A Jewish man?"

"No, ma'am," I said. "No, Aunt Sue. Now, this may be shocking news to you. Are you sitting down?"

"Yes, Elizabeth. Do tell me!"

"Well, I'm dating a woman. I'm a lesbian."

Ten of the longest seconds of my life went by. I was terrified she would say something judgmental or hang up on me.

Aunt Sue surprised me and said, "Oh, well…, I guess you don't want to meet Andrew, then."

We both laughed merrily. I was so relieved that she rolled with my news.

"Oh, well, sure. I'll meet him for lunch. Maybe we can be friends."

Aunt Sue continued, "Well, honey, have you told your parents?"

"Yes, Aunt Sue. It's been awful. They are horrified and won't let me come home for Christmas."

"What? That's terrible! Well, you come out to Houston and spend Christmas with your Uncle Bill and me, and your Dalton cousins. You are not going to spend Christmas alone!"

"Thank you so much, Aunt Sue. I'd love to."

"And I'm gonna call your daddy tomorrow morning. I'll say,

'Brothuh, shame on you! Elizabeth is your daughter, and you should love her no matter what!'"

"Thanks, Aunt Sue. But I don't think that will change his mind."

"Well, I want him to know that I do not approve of how he's treating his daughter. He doesn't have to accept your lifestyle, but it is wrong to reject you like this."

Aunt Sue did call Daddy the next day and gave him a lecture on unconditional love. He was furious at me for coming out to his sister and her family.

I felt supported and loved by Aunt Sue, Uncle Bill, and their sons and their families. I was grateful to Aunt Sue for inviting me to spend the holidays with them. I had a wonderful visit with them in Houston that year.

My experience of coming out to Aunt Liber was very different from my experience with Aunt Frannie and Aunt Sue. Aunt Liber was Mama's oldest sister. She was opinionated, conservative in a proper, old school, established Episcopalian way. And Aunt Liber was certainly no feminist. When her only son, Lanny, married a liberal, hippy, California gal, it took Aunt Liber a while to adjust.

Several years after I came out to Mama, I went to visit her and my aunts at Southern Comfort in Tennessee. Mama and I argued so much that I couldn't stay in the house after the first night. I stayed with my cousin, Rita, a few blocks down the road, in a house she had rented for her and her teenage daughters.

One afternoon, I had the coming-out talk with Aunt Liber on the porch at Southern Comfort. Mama and Aunt Frannie had gone out to lunch. I took a deep breath and said,

"Well, Aunt Liber, you probably know that Mama and I are having terrible conflict right now. I don't know if she or Aunt Frannie have told you, but I want you to know that I'm a lesbian."

Aunt Liber took a huge gulp of her scotch, followed by a deep drag from her Winston cigarette. I remember the hum of the ceiling fan and the color of her tangerine toenails peeking out from her hot pink sandals. I began to get a stomachache. I intuitively knew what was coming.

"Yes, honey, your Mama told me. She's very angry and disappointed in you."

"I know, Aunt Liber. And she's so judgmental and homophobic. She's furious that I've come out to so many family members. So, how does this news land with you?"

"Well, baby girl. I'm a traditional Southern lady! And I believe in the wisdom of the Scriptures."

I was prepared to have Aunt Liber quote the verse about homosexuality being an abomination. To my surprise, Aunt Liber went in a different direction. She was on her third scotch, and I was having my first and only one.

With great authority, Aunt Liber proclaimed,

"Darlin, the Bible says that um... well, it says somewhere that the penis fits perfectly into the vagina, like the hand fits into a glove. That's the natural way."

I was taking a sip of scotch as she said this and nearly choked in shock. This was so awkward and wrong on so many levels. I am not a Bible scholar, but I knew there was no part of scripture that described heterosexual intercourse.

"Aunt Liber, we need to agree to disagree."

"Elizabeth, darlin, you are being influenced by those unattractive, biscuit-faced feminists!"

"What on earth does that mean?"

"You know, those ugly, overweight women libbers who can't get a man. They have acne scars on their faces. That's why we call 'em biscuit faced."

"Aunt Liber, stop judging single feminists who aren't thin. I'm offended by your judgmental, heterosexist remarks."

"Lord, have mercy, child! Those radical, Yankee feminists have brain-washed you!"

"I guess we better talk about something else, Aunt Liber. I didn't know you were so conservative and judgmental."

"Well, our generation is like that. If it helps, I told your Mama that it doesn't do any good trying to get your child to change. I don't think that changed her mind. I hope y'all can come to a place of peace, darlin. I love you, and so does your Mama."

"I love you, too, Aunt Liber."

It was easier to accept Aunt Liber's limitations and homophobia than it was my mother's. I felt proud of myself for coming out to all my aunts.

To my delight, Aunt Frannie, Aunt Liber, and Aunt Sue overcame their reservations and judgments about having a lesbian niece. I continued to have positive relationships with all three of my aunts. In fact, all of them met Marie and loved her.

CHAPTER 7

The Lesbian Law of Attraction

I spent most of my thirties in my personal life in therapy working on accepting myself, dealing with my family's rejection of me, and exploring dating women and lesbian culture. I learned a great deal about how different this was from heterosexual culture.

In the lesbian culture in DC, I saw ex-partners still being best friends, the U-Haul culture of moving in after three dates, and all the different lesbian identities. I discovered there were different looks or identities, such as soft butch, stone butch (women who don't want to be touched), androgynous, jocks, hard-femmes, sporty femmes, and lipstick lesbians. Lipstick lesbian was an identity that fit me–the girly-girl type who loves to wear lipstick, eye make-up, and dress in a more feminine, sometimes even glamorous way.

Having lost most of my family, I had hoped to find a strong sense of belonging and sisterhood within the lesbian community. But I didn't feel I fit into the lesbian culture. I didn't look butch, nor did I play softball, golf, or pool. I was tired of lesbians telling me I couldn't be a real lesbian because I looked straight. Even when I sang in the Lesbian and Gay Chorus in Washington DC, several lesbians ridiculed me for wearing make-up and nail polish. Some lesbian feminists accused me of benefitting from the privilege of passing for straight. They also told me I was giving in to the heterosexist patriarchal definitions of femininity. I felt judged and angry. The irony is that I had been a feminist for almost a decade, which included marching for ERA and attending feminist consciousness-raising book groups with NOW, the National Organization for Women. I didn't understand why so many lesbians judged me so harshly. Once again, I couldn't find my tribe, my people, which left me feeling confused, rejected, and lonely.

I was almost ready to give up on women, or at least take a break from dating. I was tired of being disappointed and heartbroken in lesbian relationships. I decided to consult my astrologist, Alice. I'd been seeing her for years. She was always spot on, positive, spiritual, and practical. I liked that she was also a realtor. She was grounded in both worlds.

I knew that a few sessions with Alice would be a good opportunity to update my chart and focus on my career. We looked at my chart. Alice said things looked promising for new clients and possibly a new love. I was skeptical and doubtful about that last bit and told her so. She suggested we do a Tarot card reading.

Alice said, "Elizabeth, look at these cards. We have the High Priestess and the Lover cards, which tell us the energy is right for you to manifest your ideal partner. Be very specific and make a list of 100 qualities you want in a partner. Do a ritual and have a friend witness it. Allow the Universe to respond."

At first, I thought I'd never be able to list 100 qualities. Keeping an open mind, I picked up my journal, meditated a while, then the words began to flow from my heart to my pen and onto the page. Here are a few highlights from that list:

- Very out lesbian
- Sexy
- Intelligent
- Sporty, soft Butch
- Professional
- Classic dresser
- No tattoos or body piercings
- Spiritual, not religious
- Loves theatre and storytelling
- Has done several years of therapy
- Loves international travel
- Oh, and has at least one dead parent! (I'd lost my father by this point and wanted to find someone who understood and experienced grief.)

Within about twenty-five minutes, I had completed my list of 100 qualities I wanted in an ideal partner.

What helped me believe I deserved love was a decision to love myself first. The process started with a couple of commitments. I committed to loving all parts of myself, especially the difficult parts I had previously rejected, such as my abandoned inner child and my inner critic. I also committed to believing I was worthy of receiving love with someone who was emotionally present. I developed a mindfulness meditation practice. Before long, I began experiencing true forgiveness. I forgave myself for my own contribution to my past failed relationships. Next, I focused on forgiving my family members and former partners for the parts they played, even if we no longer had relationships. As part of loving all parts of myself, I released the notion I had to be perfect in some way and replaced that self-talk with a "good-enough" attitude. From that point, I permitted myself to risk again and began telling my closest friends about the list I was making of one hundred ideal qualities I was seeking in a partner. One of these friends helped me perform a spiritual ritual to help me find this ideal woman, and I asked the Divine Feminine, the Goddess, to help me manifest the right partner, at the right time.

On New Year's Eve, I went to my best friend's house. We lit candles around the altar, and I said my favorite Goddess invocation (By this point, I'd left the Episcopal Church):

Oh, Great Mother Goddess Divine.

Help me manifest my lesbian lover so fine.

Bring her to me, all in your time.

Help me receive her and make her all mine!

That night, I dreamed I met my soulmate–a redheaded, Scottish-looking woman with greenish-blue eyes and a smile that lit up the room. She was kind, with a heart of gold and had an infectious laugh. I woke up feeling like my life was about to change. I was open to possibilities and tried not to be attached to the outcome.

The next weekend, I went to a good, old-fashioned, lesbian potluck. After my previous bisexual polyamorous potluck adventure, I was hoping this potluck would be a bit calmer. But how much hummus can lesbians eat? Garlic, red pepper, lemon, and black bean hummus accompanied by trays and trays of crackers, pizza, cupcakes, and brownies were washed down with iced tea, Budweiser, and Diet Coke. No fine Southern hospitality here! I went without knowing a soul there. Chalk it up to another adventurous lesbian-seeking mission. The party was held in a modest 1950s ranch-style home in Fairfax, Virginia. I walked in and scanned the living room. Make no mistake; I was staring at a group of older, retired, military lesbians. I was thirty-seven, and most of the women looked like they were over fifty-five. I appreciated their service, but they were not my type.

The year was 2001, before online dating and Meetup groups became popular. Back in those days, lesbians met in bars, bookstores, through personal ads in the *Washington Blade* (DC's gay newspaper), Home Depot, and, of course, all those wonderful potluck dinners.

After standing around for an hour talking to retired Army colonels, I was ready to go home. Then, the door opened and in walked the striking redhead with those sparkling, greenish-blue eyes. I recognized her at once as the woman from my dream! How could I manage to contain my excitement in front of this woman I had actually manifested? I had to keep my cool as she headed straight to me. Our eyes locked and she said, "Hi there! I'm Marie. Nice to meet you!"

"Hello, Marie. I'm Elizabeth. You have a Southern accent! Where are you from?"

"Yes, I'm from Raleigh, North Carolina. Go Wolfpack! You sound like you're from way down South."

"Yeah, Marie. I'm from a tiny town in northeast Mississippi, called Okolona, near Tupelo. I call myself a recoverin' belle from a long line of unrecovered belles. Bless their hearts."

Ah, the flirting had begun. We sat down on the couch and talked for almost two hours. Marie and I were from similar worlds. She spoke my language with her gentle Southern drawl, a familiar cadence that warmed my heart and felt like home. We both understood the eccentricities of Southern culture–like sittin' on the porch for hours telling and listening to stories while sippin' sweet tea, recognizing our mamas' passive-aggressive behavior, and knowing all the different meanings of the phrase, "Bless your heart."

There's the "bless your heart" in sympathy said after someone has the flu. There's the empathic tone of this phrase said after someone's mother died. Then, the bless *her* heart followed by "she gained 40 pounds after her divorce, and during… menopause" muttered in a scornful or judgmental tone.

Marie and I agreed we shared a conflicted relationship with the South. We talked about loving Southern hospitality, our slower pace of savoring life, and fine Southern writers, especially our contemporary Southern lesbian writers like Rita Mae Brown and Dorothy Allison. We agreed we hated the homophobia, racism, and sexism.

I decided to ask some probing questions. I'm a Scorpio, so I like to go deep. I cannot tolerate superficial small talk at a party. After so many painful lesbian relationships, I wanted to be careful before I considered opening my heart again.

"So, Marie, are you out? Are your parents still living?"

"Yeah, I'm out. I've been out to my family for many years. They accept me. I still have my dad, but I lost my mom two years ago, and that was the hardest time of my life. She died of a heart attack in the same rocking chair she rocked me in as a baby. I saw a therapist twice a week for a long time."

"Oh, Marie, I'm so sorry to hear that."

Yes! A double hitter! Therapy and a dead parent!

We exchanged numbers, and I called Marie the next day. We had our first date five days later, which lasted until 3:00 am. We spoke each other's language as only two Southern lesbians can do. There was hot chemistry and no ex in her life! I felt I had found my soulmate.

And indeed, I had. As of this writing, we have been together for nineteen years. Eleven years ago, we got married in San Francisco before the big rainbow wave of gay marriage throughout the US. I will never forget that day. I wondered how Mama and Daddy would have reacted. Their youngest daughter was now finally and legally married.

CHAPTER 8

Learning to Let Go

It still hurts to remember how horrified my parents were when I came out to them. I knew they would struggle with my news, but I was shocked by their anger and cruelty. I knew Daddy would shun me, but I thought Mama might be more accepting. Before I came out, she used to visit me several times a year in DC After I came out to her, she never came to visit me again. I had hoped she would have a change of heart, eventually.

As you know, I didn't have the courage to come out directly to Daddy. Mama told him six months after I came out to her. Daddy told me no one in our family wanted to be around me and that I should move to another country. When I called home once, he answered the phone and said, "I have nothing to say to you. Here's your mother." I was furious and devastated by his rejection.

I tried to visit my parents for two years after I came out, but Mama kept telling me Daddy wasn't ready to see me. So, I convinced Mama to meet me for a spiritual weekend at a labyrinth workshop at an Episcopal church in Richmond. We both loved walking labyrinths as a form of meditation. I had hoped that long meditative walks on the labyrinth would help us heal. A labyrinth is an ancient symbol that relates to wholeness. It is a patterned circular path used as a walking meditation or spiritual practice. Walking the labyrinth represents our own spiritual journey to let go of our struggles step by step and embrace our connection with the Divine.

Mama and I had separate rooms at the Holiday Inn, but we met over dinner that Saturday night in Richmond's fashionable downtown dining hub, Shockoe Slip.

I asked Mama what it would take for her to stop judging me and accept that I was a lesbian. She looked at me with a hardened frown and squinted her dark, brown eyes as she whispered across the table.

"There is nothing that will ever make me accept this sinful lifestyle you live. I will never believe that this is who you are."

My response was pure rage. I wasn't ready to feel the grief.

"I can't believe how judgmental and mean you are being, Mama. I had hoped you could eventually be happy that I'm happy being my authentic self."

"No, I'll never approve of you. You're making a terrible mistake."

For the rest of that weekend, I was miserable. We finished the labyrinth workshop, and I did feel somewhat more peaceful from walking the labyrinth, but Mama and I were still engaged in a power struggle.

Unfortunately, in 1997, only one year later, I received some shocking news about Daddy and Mama. They were in Boston visiting my sister and her family. It was around midnight on a Friday night, and I had gotten home from a friend's 40th birthday party when my phone rang. I knew immediately it was bad news. It was my sister, Marguerite, who hadn't called me in over a year. I intuitively knew that a tragedy had happened. I nervously answered the phone.

"Hello?"

"Hi Elizabeth, it's Marguerite. I have some bad news. Daddy died from a heart attack here in Boston. We were at a church dinner. He went to the men's room and was gone for about thirty minutes. We sent our friend, who is a doctor, into the restroom to check on him. Daddy was lying on the floor unconscious. He died at the hospital."

I was stunned and burst into tears. My sister continued, "We were still in the waiting room when Mama started holding her head in her hands, screaming out in pain, saying she was having a migraine. It turns out she had a massive stroke and is now in a coma. You should fly up here in the morning."

I was in shock. Daddy was dead, and I hadn't seen him in two years. We had never reconciled.

Getting that phone call at midnight from my sister telling me all this tragic news was horrific. I felt like I'd lost both of my parents at once. Mama was in a coma for several days at Massachusetts General Hospital. Meanwhile, my siblings and I had to plan Daddy's funeral in our hometown of Okolona, Mississippi, from Boston without Mama. We knew she couldn't attend his funeral, which was heartbreaking.

After I returned to the DC area from Daddy's funeral in my hometown, I checked the mail and discovered a letter Mama had written me the day before she and Daddy traveled to Boston, which was the day before he died. Mama had suggested that I come home for Thanksgiving since it had been over two years since I had been home to visit. She said she thought Daddy was beginning to soften his heart towards me. It was bittersweet reading her letter. I'll never know what might have been.

The situation was made even worse by my estranged relationship with my siblings. For the first seven years after I came out, two of my siblings refused to meet any of my girlfriends. (I had several short but significant relationships during that period.) My sister, Marguerite, told me that she thought my "lifestyle" was wrong and that she thought the stress of my coming-out process caused our parents' health problems. Her opinion was giving me too much power. I was stunned and hurt by her judgments of me and by her homophobia.

For years, I carried resentment, anger, and hurt towards my parents and siblings–especially towards Mama. She was the one person who had loved me unconditionally as a child. I kept waiting for her to have a change of heart and apologize for judging and rejecting me and refusing to meet Marie. Unfortunately, that day also never came.

It had been five years since Mama's first stroke, and I hadn't seen her in almost two years. I tried to visit her in Boston, where she lived with my sister and her family, but there were always excuses from them about why it wasn't a good time for me to visit. Then I had a dream that Mama was going to die soon. I pay attention to those kinds of prophetic dreams about people dying because this has happened to me several times before.

I decided to visit Mama that summer at Southern Comfort in the mountains of Tennessee, where she would be spending the summer with her sisters. This was a huge step for me. I had not been allowed to visit that house or my childhood home in Mississippi for eight years. So, this meant I hadn't seen Aunt Liber, Aunt Frannie, or any of my cousins in almost a decade. I missed feeling connected to my extended family and decided I needed to tell Mama that I longed to see her and the rest of our family. She reluctantly agreed to let me come if I would not bring Marie, who had been my partner for a year and a half at that point. I was disappointed but decided to stop trying to change Mama. I tried to release any expectations about how I would be treated. Intuitively, I felt this would likely be the last visit I would have with Mama in person, and I wanted to have some healing with her. It wasn't easy.

I remember walking into Southern Comfort, our beloved Victorian family summer mountain home. Mama, my aunts, my cousins, and my sister were sitting on the wrap-around porch that breezy July afternoon. It felt strange seeing everyone. Everyone hugged and greeted me, but it felt like no one knew what to say. No one acknowledged it had been eight long years since I'd been to Southern Comfort. No one said they had missed me.

Then my elderly Aunt Frannie slowly walked over to me. She hugged me, held me close, and said, "Darlin, it's so great to see you again. I love you so much."

I was touched by Aunt Frannie's love and affection. And yet I longed for Mama to say those words. I kept reminding myself that I didn't have expectations or regrets, but I did.

I wanted Mama to throw her arms around me, hold me close, and say, "Oh, my dear Elizabeth, I'm so sorry I've been so cold and cruel. I'm so sorry we've lost so many years. We could have resolved this long ago. Please forgive me."

But she didn't say any tender words. She was still a bit frail from her stroke. She hugged me tentatively and said she was glad I had arrived safely. The two of us went to dinner that night at a local Mexican restaurant. That night, I ran into my favorite English teacher, Susan Core, from the boarding school I had graduated from five miles down the road. We greeted each other briefly. I pretended I was having a normal visit with Mama, but nothing felt normal.

Mama couldn't read the menu, a lingering effect from her stroke. Even though the stroke had happened several years earlier, I wasn't used to seeing her so impaired. She walked slower and was always afraid she would fall. She was seventy-seven, but she seemed eighty-seven. She could no longer drive. It felt like a role reversal in which I was the mother. Not only was I shocked and saddened by her limitations, I was also angry the stroke had hijacked my mother and left a shell of her previous vibrant, healthy self.

Mama and I went to breakfast at the Waffle House that Sunday morning. She asked how I was, and if I still sang in my church choir. I told her I no longer sang in that choir, nor did I attend that Episcopal church anymore, but I enjoyed singing in the Lesbian and Gay Chorus in DC with Marie.

Mama got a stern look on her face as if she tasted spoiled milk. She leaned across the table and whispered in an angry tone, "I told you that I don't want to hear about that part of your life."

I decided to ask her a question I'd been wondering about for many years.

"Mama, what's the hardest thing about having a lesbian daughter?"

With a scowl on her face, she again whispered, "People make fun of people like you."

I was stunned, but I heard her message loud and clear. My mother was ashamed of having a lesbian daughter. Damn, that hurt. I made my way to the restroom to give myself a moment.

Then something amazing and unexpected happened. The lights suddenly went out in the restroom. It was pitch black. I took a few deep breaths to ground myself. I received an intuitive message that I perceived as a spiritual message from the Divine. (Although I no longer identified as a traditional Christian, I still believe in a Higher Power.) I felt a feminine presence in that dark restroom. I like to call her the Great Mother. Her energy felt very loving and maternal.

In my mind, I heard this message:

"Your mother is wounded. She has limited consciousness. She's not going to change. She does love you, but she feels rejected and betrayed by you. Remember that she's not comfortable with her own sexuality, much less yours. You no longer need her approval. You are good enough. You are living as your authentic self. You can let go of your suffering and wanting your mother to change. Let go of her and move on, dear one."

And I then felt an inner peace expand from my heart. I knew, at a soul level, I no longer needed my mother's approval. How freeing that was. I could accept her limitations, which brought me a sense of relief. Although it was a bit awkward, I enjoyed the rest of the day with Mama at church. Later that afternoon, we went to a music concert with my sister and her husband, in which my fourteen-year-old niece played her violin. I was glad I stayed at a hotel for this visit, which helped me have better boundaries with Mama and gave me a break from the rest of the family. Several two- or three-hour visits with Mama was so much better than spending three full days with her with no breaks.

Six months later, on a rainy Tuesday night in January, I received a difficult phone call from my brother-in-law, Sam, my sister's husband.

"Elizabeth, I have some sad news for you. Your mother has had another stroke—a massive one. She's in a coma in ICU at Massachusetts General Hospital. It's a huge bleed in her brain. The doctor says she won't recover. Y'all have some hard decisions to make as siblings. You should get a flight up here tomorrow morning."

It's odd to think about the details we remember right before or as we learn about a life-changing event. It was about five-thirty in the afternoon and already dark. I was at Marie's condo. We were about to have dinner at our new friends' house, a gay male couple. Marie called them and told them what happened. Momentarily, I felt a tiny bit disappointed about our cancelation and wondered what would happen to that budding friendship. (We never saw them again, which is typical for the fast-paced DC area.) I remember thinking my life was about to change drastically. I knew Mama would die within a few days.

The next morning Marie and I flew to Boston. It was awkward that Marie was meeting my brother Jem, and my sister, Marguerite, at the hospital for the first time. She had met my brother, Reynolds, and his wife, Karoyl, briefly over dinner in Mississippi the previous year.

Stranger still was the fact that Marie met my mother as she lay unconscious in a coma, less than forty-eight hours away from her death. It seemed surreal–like a nightmare. The two women I loved the most would never have the opportunity to know one another. I felt helpless with so many wild emotions moving through me–shock, sadness, anger, and regret. I knew that becoming an orphan at thirty-nine was going to be hard–so hard.

So many memories of Mama flooded my mind. I remembered how she rocked me and sang to me when I was a child. Then there were our trips to Europe, the Grand Canyon, California, Mexico, Montreal, and Tennessee during my teenage and twenty-something years. There were the Episcopal retreats and literature conferences we went to in North Carolina, and our conversations about her childhood in her beloved Mississippi Delta home in Indianola in the 1920s and 30s. I'll never forget our lively discussions about the importance of embracing the Divine Feminine within the patriarchal religion of Christianity.

As a teenager, I sometimes felt smothered by my mother. I did my fair share of rebelling by drinking and dating a few wild fellows. I regret that I was sometimes sarcastic with her and quite critical of her for not having a career and for not being a feminist. I didn't understand why she stayed in such an unhappy marriage.

The truth was that Marguerite Cooper McCain, my mother, was a complicated, private woman who was sweet, gentle, introverted, and sometimes manipulative, homophobic, and often passive-aggressive. Her generation of women was taught to please people, submit to men, and pretend everything was lovely. She had rejected the feminist movement, which threatened her because she was financially dependent on her husband.

She often said, "Well, I'm no radical man-hating feminist. I guess I'm a 'soft-shelled feminist' 'cause I know how to treat men with respect and attention. But in the end, I know how to get my way. I let your Daddy think he's the boss, but I'm the one controlling most things."

I knew beneath Mama's fear, anger, and hurt, that she loved me deeply. I think she felt like she lost me when I came out. I've thought a great deal about this. When a straight daughter loves a man, usually the emotional bond continues with her mother if there was one. But when a lesbian daughter loves another woman, this can be threatening for a heterosexual mother because she knows that she is no longer the most important woman in her daughter's life. A grieving process needs to happen. Unfortunately, Mama got stuck in the anger and disapproval stage. I'll never know if she ever allowed herself to grieve the loss of our relationship.

As I walked into her hospital room, I was shocked and saddened by what I saw. Mama had no ruby red lipstick on, and her hair was a dirty mess. Her hands and arms were bruised and swollen from the lack of circulation. Tubes went into her nose, and her chest struggled up and down with the sound of the oxygen machine. That sound of her labored breathing haunted me for years.

I was grateful for the few minutes I had to spend alone with her. It felt poignant that she brought me into this world and that I was witnessing her leaving this world.

I gently leaned in and said, "Mama, it's Elizabeth, your baby, here. I'm so sorry we've had such a hard time with each other. I want you to know how much I love you. I know you love me. Thank you for being my mother. I forgive you and hope you forgive me. It's

okay for you to let go. You'll be with Daddy and your parents. I'll
miss you. You did a good job here. Now it's time for you to move on."

Then I sang this song to her (written by Libby Roderick),

> *How could anyone ever tell you,*
>
> *You were anything less than beautiful.*
>
> *How could anyone ever tell you,*
>
> *You were less than whole.*
>
> *How can anyone fail to notice,*
>
> *That your loving is a miracle,*
>
> *How deeply you're connected to my soul.*

Big tears streamed down Mama's cheeks. The nurse said that
was because she had just given her eye drops. Although she was
unconscious in a coma, I knew on a soul level she heard me and
was touched.

Standing by my sister, Marguerite, on Mama's left side, we
watched her take her final, long, slow breath, a few minutes after the
nurse turned off the oxygen. I felt the energy of her soul hover above
us. I could feel her love for us, all four of her children. The spouses
and Marie (who was not yet my spouse) stood by the door respectfully
watching us. I could see Mama in my mind's eye, wearing her royal
blue, ultra-suede suit that she liked to wear to church in the winter.

With her ruby red Revlon lipstick, perfectly applied, she looked
lovingly upon us and said, "Oh, my four babies. I hate to leave you…
They're having a welcoming party for me in heaven and I need to go
greet everyone. Remember how much I love you all and know that
I'm always in your heart. Take care of each other."

My oldest brother, Jem, fell into my arms sobbing for about ten
seconds. We'd hugged maybe twice in my life before this, so this was
a touching and promising moment. I hoped we could connect with
each other through our grief, but the moment passed.

CHAPTER 9

My Journey with Marie

By this point in my life, Marie had become an important figure, so it's only fitting that I tell you a little more about my soulmate and life partner who stood by me through this entire ordeal.

I knew there was something special about Marie that first night we met at the potluck. Our eyes met the moment she walked in the door. After the initial shock of remembering her from my dream, I recognized her from the weekend before when I went to a lesbian singles dinner at a Mexican restaurant called Anita's in Falls Church, Virginia. She had caught my eye there because she was a cute redhead with a sporty, short haircut and sparkling, greenish-blue eyes. Even then, I had noticed her soft Southern accent and her NC State sweatshirt. What threw me though was that she came to that dinner with two handsome men. It was a dinner for single lesbians. What the hell were those guys doing there? I was confused. They looked gay with their hairstyles full of plenty of product, and their jeans with tight black t-shirts that revealed their muscular bodies. They were seated at a table in front of me, so I was facing Marie and these guys. They laughed in an intimate, expressive way; the way close friends do who've known each other for years. When someone asked Marie where she lived, I heard her say, "We live at Cambridge Court Condominiums in Arlington."

Upon hearing this, I wondered if Marie was bisexual or polyamorous.

We smiled at each other from across the room that night, but we didn't officially meet and talk to each other until that next weekend at the lesbian potluck of mostly retired military women.

When Marie and I sat down to talk, it didn't take long for me to ask her who the two guys were who had gone with her to the lesbian dinner the week before.

Marie explained, "Oh, those guys, Mark and Kevin, they are my gay friends. We go everywhere together. I love them. We are family to one another. She later proclaimed that it was sometimes easier for her to be friends with gay men than it was to be friends with lesbians. She explained, "There's no sexual attraction with gay guys. They're more fun, and there's no drama. After my last break-up with my former partner, I decided to take a break from dating women and have fun with my gay boyfriends."

I thought this was a refreshing attitude. It made me wish I had a posse of gay boys with whom I could have fun.

Our relationship started quickly. I was the pursuer. I called Marie on a Sunday afternoon, the day after we met. I left her a voicemail message—something like, "Hi, Marie. This is Elizabeth. It was so great to talk to you last night. I think we have a lot in common. So, um, I was wondering if you might want to have dinner sometime soon? I'm around this afternoon and tonight, so call me. Bye."

I made sure I spoke in my slow, sultry Southern accent to be sexy. She returned my call that January night around 8:00 pm. We talked until midnight. We shared our coming out stories, our family stories, and made sure we didn't share any of the same exes. Luckily, we didn't.

Our first date was four days later, on a Thursday night, at the Evening Star restaurant in Alexandria, Virginia. Marie wore a peach-colored sweater, black jeans, cowboy boots, and a gray trench coat. I wore a black sweater, black jeans, black suede boots, and my purple down jacket. It was a frigid, rainy night. After an intimate dinner over pasta and white wine, we sat in her navy-blue Saab and talked about our careers and made out until 3:00 am. We had a strong emotional and physical attraction. We saw each other once a week for dates–usually on a Friday or Saturday night for the next month. By Valentine's Day, which was also the weekend she graduated from massage therapy school, we decided we would date each other exclusively. I showed up at her graduation at a Unitarian Church with yellow roses to seal our courtship. (It was too soon for red ones.)

There has always been an inviting warmth about Marie that has helped me feel nurtured and safe. Her bright eyes, warm smile, and gentle Southern drawl opened my heart to love again. Most of the women I dated were from the East Coast. (Oh, there was one woman I had dated who was from Florida, but that's not the real South.) I knew that dating a woman who was also Southern was a powerful connection. We shared our conflicted emotions and perspectives on the South.

I was also drawn to Marie because she had been out as a lesbian for over twenty years. I had only been out for seven years. She knew she was gay when she was in junior high school, when she had her first girlfriend. Her parents accepted her sexuality, even though they had grown up Baptist. We both had an older brother who was a fundamentalist Christian. In fact, Marie's brother was a Pentecostal minister. She had been able to set boundaries with him and the rest of her family about not talking about religion. I was relieved to discover that, like me, Marie was more spiritual than religious.

I learned that Marie was a licensed professional engineer at a reputable engineering firm. She also had a degree in Forestry and had a passion for trees and all of nature. She was, and is, more analytical and athletic than me. She balances my more emotionally dramatic personality.

I wanted to share my spiritual interests with Marie–things like Goddess and the moon circles I attended, as well as meditation retreats. I was worried she would think I was too "woo-woo." She was definitely more mainstream than me. To my surprise, Marie went with me to moon circles, and occasionally to St. Mark's Episcopal Church, where I had come out seven years earlier. I no longer identified as a Christian, but I still felt connected to the St. Mark's community.

Marie was fun, extroverted, and curious about science and history, which also intrigued me. And we had a mutual interest in haunted places and ghosts. I also loved that Marie had a rich alto voice. I'm a second soprano, so it is a pleasure to sing with her. For almost three years, Marie and I enjoyed singing together in the Lesbian and Gay Chorus in DC . We also participated together in community theater on Capitol Hill for several summers. We performed in gay and lesbian versions of Gilbert and Sullivan musicals, comic operettas, such as *Iolanthe* and the *Mikado*. We had developed strong friendships with other lesbian couples in our performing arts communities.

After Mama died, things shifted and got harder. I didn't have the energy to sing in the chorus that year. Most of our friends had not lost a parent yet. Marie had lost her mother, but still had her father, whom I'd known and loved.

My private practice as a therapist was smaller. I didn't have the energy to do marketing to get new clients. I was tired of the stress and expense of the DC area. I decided to do a radical thing and move to the beautiful mountains of Asheville, North Carolina, without a job. Luckily, I had about six months' worth of savings. I wanted to slow down and heal from the grief of my mother's death. I asked Marie to move to Asheville with me. She said she would if she could get a job. I moved to Asheville in May 2004. It was hard to move without Marie, but my soul knew I needed to be in Asheville. We continued our long distance relationship and saw each other every three weeks, but it was hard. I didn't know anyone in Asheville when I moved there. I decided to delay starting a counseling practice so that I could do some healing and personal growth work. I quickly found a spiritual community, Venus Rising, near Asheville, that offered training in shamanic breathwork. That spiritual community, led by Linda Starwolf and her late husband, Brad Collins, helped me get grounded to continue my healing process through grief.

Marie moved to Asheville by that August. It was the first time we lived together, almost three years after we met. It was stressful because we have different approaches to keeping a household. Marie is very neat and organized. I'm messy and disorganized. And we are both controlling. Fortunately, we found a skilled therapist and got help to resolve our conflict.

A few days after Marie arrived, we embarked on an adventurous Goddess trip to England and Scotland that September. The next year, we went on a transformational shamanic trip to Egypt with the Venus Rising community and spiritual teacher, Nikki Scully. Forty spiritual healers from all over the country went to the ancient temples and tombs of Egypt, as well as the Great Pyramid of Giza.

For the next couple of years, Marie and I enjoyed living in Asheville. I had a small counseling practice and attended an energy healing school. Marie got a job as an engineer for the city. We had made some good friendships. But her job didn't pay well. We missed the sophistication of living in a large metropolitan area. We noticed that many lesbians in Asheville were closeted. We missed good theater, museums, and having access to a large

LGBTQ culture. So, we decided to move back to the DC area. Marie landed a stable government job that paid better than her city job in Asheville. I started over with my private practice in the Maryland suburbs. We reconnected with some of our DC lesbian friends. We were sad to leave Asheville, but we were ready for city life again.

In 2008, a year after we moved back to the DC area, I proposed to Marie. This was before gay marriage was legalized throughout the country. Unfortunately, I didn't plan a romantic proposal. I was commuting to Berkeley, California, for an interfaith seminary I was attending at the Chaplaincy Institute. Marie and I were thinking of moving to the Bay area. A gay classmate of mine, Doug, had gotten married. He talked about how his marriage to his partner strengthened their relationship. This was right before gay marriage was voted down in California. But Doug was firm in his belief that his marriage was the best thing that had happened to him. He also believed that we would have gay marriage throughout the country within five years. I wanted to feel the same kind of security and belief that gay marriage would soon be legal throughout the country.

I knew I loved Marie and felt like she was my soulmate for life. In fact, Marie and I had discussed the possibility of having a commitment ceremony. (The words "gay marriage" were not yet in our vocabulary.) We had been taking a class on community and faith at St. Mark's Episcopal Church. When we approached the priest to discuss the possibility of having a commitment ceremony, he told us we could not use any prayers from the Book of Common Prayer because that was only for married heterosexual people. He added that although he knew this wasn't fair, he could not disobey the bishop and go against the church's policy. Marie and I were hurt and felt discriminated against. This put a damper on having a commitment ceremony. So, we dropped that idea.

On a Sunday afternoon in July, after reading an article in *The Washington Post* about how if gay marriage ever happened legally, we would have 1,148 federal rights, I did something impulsive. I had been reading the newspaper in my office. Marie was watching a baseball game in the kitchen. I ran into the kitchen, looked at her, and announced,

"Marie, we should get married in San Francisco in October before gay marriage in California is voted out in November. Let's do it!"

I excitedly awaited Marie's response.

There was a long pause. My heart started to sink, as Marie frowned, and said, "Elizabeth, marriage is for straight people."

I was disappointed and shocked by her response. Instead of making myself vulnerable, I got angry and said, "What? Are you saying you don't want to marry me?"

Marie fired back and said, "Well, this isn't a romantic proposal at all."

Conflict had again entered our relationship. We entered couple's therapy again and began a long exploration of what it meant to each of us to get married. We learned so much about each other's ideas and fears of a lifetime commitment. Within a couple of weeks, Marie was ready to be "engaged."

Because we were getting married far away in San Francisco, we decided to only invite my friends and professors from my interfaith seminary program and my lesbian cousin, Jamie, and her then partner, who lived in Burbank, California at that time. We planned our ceremony and wrote our own vows with the help of a spiritual mentor. Barb, a lesbian friend and classmate of mine from The Chaplaincy Institute, was our wedding officiant.

On a sunny fall afternoon on October 14, 2008, we married in the beautiful City Hall of San Francisco. The rules of the courthouse insisted that we could not have music or chairs, which felt odd. Thirteen people attended. My cousin, Jamie, was my best woman.

Marie's best woman was Jamie's partner at that time, Susan. Marie
wore a beautiful cobalt blue silk suit. She chose to wear a skirt rather
than pants and black pumps. I wore a fuchsia silk blouse and a black
silk skirt with black pumps. We found an Irish jeweler in Berkeley,
who designed and made our gold wedding bands, with a Celtic Tree
of Life design. We each carried a beautiful bouquet of roses. Marie's
was deep red, and mine was fuchsia.

My favorite reading from our wedding was a poem by E. E.
Cummings, [i carry your heart with me(i carry it in]

> *i carry your heart with me (i carry it in*
> *my heart) i am never without it (anywhere*
> *i go you go, my dear; and whatever is done*
> *by only me is your doing, my darling)*
> > *i fear*
> *no fate (for you are my fate, my sweet) i want*
> *no world (for beautiful you are my world, my true)*
> *and it's you are whatever a moon has always meant*
> *and whatever a sun will always sing is you*
>
> *here is the deepest secret nobody knows*
> *(here is the root of the root and the bud of the bud*
> *and the sky of the sky of a tree called life; which grows*
> *higher than soul can hope or mind can hide)*
> *and this is the wonder that's keeping the stars apart*
>
> *i carry your heart (i carry it in my heart).*

It was a moving service on an upper floor of San Francisco's stunningly gorgeous City Hall. We had a dinner reception at an elegant Italian restaurant in San Francisco. A short trip to Santa Cruz was our honeymoon, followed by a longer one to Italy the next year.

It is not always easy to share daily life with a spouse. Our relationship has had a boatload of challenges: my mother's death, my aunts' deaths, Marie's father's death, our dog's death, selling and buying a house, menopause, growing together through Imago relationship therapy, friends' deaths, and a diminishing lesbian community.

Marie has stayed with me through it all. Even though I can be messy, dramatic, self-absorbed, anxious, and high maintenance, Marie has weathered every storm with me for the past nineteen years. This is astonishing to me. How did I get to be so lucky?

What keeps us together? Our love for one another, our ability to laugh and cry and forgive each other helps. My love for this incredible woman is boundless. I cannot imagine my life without her. Marie is my anchor, my person, and my soulmate. I'm eternally grateful for her presence in my life.

My childhood home on Monroe Avenue in Okolona, Mississippi.

Mama and Daddy

(Marguerite Cooper McCain and James Everett McCain) as young parents around 1960.

Mama holding me. Even at 6 months old, I knew I had a challenging road ahead.

I was three years old the first time I performed at Grandmother McCain's house.

Proud of Our Town

Welcome to Okolona, Mississippi. My hometown's sign in the 1940s.

A beautiful fall day at Southern Comfort in Tennessee.

My paternal grandmother, Gertrude Pinson McCain.

Aunt Frannie, Mama, and Aunt Liber preparing for their porch party at Southern Comfort.

Little Elizabeth with Aunt Liber and Aunt Frannie at Southern Comfort in 1967.

Mama and her sisters entertaining on the porch at Southern Comfort in 1967.

My maternal grandfather, "Pop" in WWI, Forrest Graham Cooper.

My maternal grandmother, Marguerite Park Cooper, "Bopie" in the 1920s.

My maternal grandparents wrote love letters during WWI. This is an image of a letter my grandmother, "Bopie," wrote to my grandfather, "Pop."

Me at sweet 16.

With my sister, Marguerite, brother, Reynolds (back, right), and the Dalton cousins at Christmas in 1969.

Mama at Grace Episcopal, my hometown church.

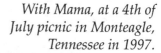

With Mama, at a 4th of July picnic in Monteagle, Tennessee in 1997.

My first trip to Provincetown, in 2001, wearing my "Lesbians for Lipstick" shirt!

With Marie at our home in Maryland.

Celebrating my 40th birthday with Marie and friends (not a lesbian potluck).

With Aunt Sue near Houston, Texas in 2010.

Mama (right) and her sisters, Aunt Liber (middle) and Aunt Frannie (left) as they got older, sitting on their favorite porch at Southern Comfort, Monteagle, Tennessee.

Mama and Daddy in 1990.

Daddy in a good mood.

Mama in Boston in 1998.

Ms. Shirley, Mama's Ole Miss sorority sister (Delta, Delta, Delta), at Mama's funeral.

Visiting Ms. Shirley at her house in Indianola, Mississippi, Easter, 2003.

A champagne toast at our wedding reception!

Marie and I were married at City Hall in San Francisco, California on October 14, 2008.

Just pronounced, "legally married!"

Ms. Dot, my P.E. teacher from All Saints Episcopal School.

Our first Olivia cruise to the Virgin Islands in 2014 to celebrate my 50th birthday.

Friends at Ms. Dot's lake house near Vicksburg, Mississippi.

Performances of A Lesbian Belle Tells… (left, Rehoboth Beach, Delaware) (right, Baltimore, Maryland).

It was a joy to be able to share my stories at Southern Comfort before we sold the home.

A fun laugh with Mr. Ham.

My teachers and classmates from St. Andrew's-Sewanee School came to see me perform my play at Southern Comfort. Followed by a porch party!

Two of my favorite teachers, Susan Core and Eugene Ham at Southern Comfort in 2017.

My dear friend, Martha.

A final shot of Southern Comfort before we sold it in 2019.

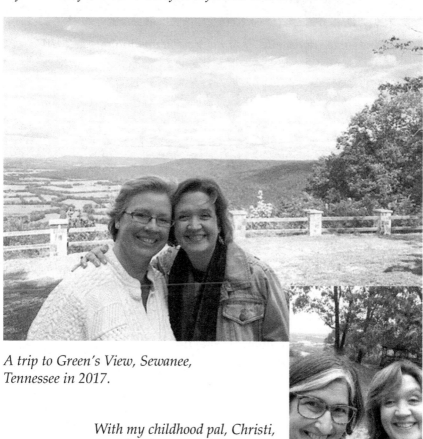

A trip to Green's View, Sewanee, Tennessee in 2017.

With my childhood pal, Christi, from Southern Comfort days, in Monteagle, Tennessee.

Fun with friends, Tanya and PJ in the Virginia mountains in 2020.

After performing with New Wave Singers of Baltimore. Eliza, Spice, Karyn, and Marie.

With my chosen sister, Lynne at a long lunch in Takoma Park, Maryland.

With my friend, Heidi, who also sings in the chorus.

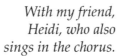

With Marie on a Shamanic trip to Ireland.

National Botanical Garden, Christmas 2019.

Mystical Ireland, 2019.

With Marie at the Women's March in Washington, DC in 2019.

CHAPTER 10

A Southern Funeral to Die For

Mama's death marked a new chapter in my life. A few days after she died in Boston, Marie and I flew down to Mississippi for her funeral. It was a traditional Episcopal funeral in my childhood church, Grace Episcopal. I remember it was a quiet service with prayers from the Book of Common Prayer and comforting hymns such as "Amazing Grace," "How Great Thou Art," and "Jerusalem, My Happy Home."

After the burial, we went back to my childhood home on Monroe Avenue for the "celebration of life party," cuz y'all, Southern funerals are to die for. That's when the healing begins. All that connecting and remembering and sharing stories for hours with friends and family. Let's face it - sometimes our friends are more fun than our family members. There are peals of laughter and soft teary eyes. Joy and sadness held in a container of love. Sharing heartwarming stories and eating comfort food–these rituals begin to heal grief.

Oh, the food. All that delicious Southern funeral food–like melt-in-your-mouth pot roast, crispy fried chicken, cooked to death casseroles of asparagus with melted Velveeta cheese on top, and homemade biscuits with ham. And the desserts: sock-it-to-me pound cake, moist chocolate cake, and apple pie. Not exactly healthy, but to Southerners, this kind of food was a staple of our lives growing up, before gluten-free was a thing. There's an amazing book called *Being Dead is No Excuse: The Official Southern Ladies Guide to Hosting the Perfect Funeral* by Gayden Metcalfe and Charlotte Hays. (There are scrumptious recipes in that book.) Most Southern funerals are overflowing with plenty of booze, but Mama left a detailed outline of her funeral, with stern instructions to not have one drop of alcohol. I was surprised by this because Mama had been a light drinker. Perhaps she was concerned that her oldest, Jem, would drink too much. You see, he's a former hippy, who later became a fundamentalist Christian and drinks like a fish. I'll never understand how that happened. My sister insisted that we follow Mama's wishes. So, we did.

Marie and I walked into the house and entered the living room. There were lots of proper church ladies in their black funeral dresses standing around. Everyone stared at us when we walked into the room.

My sister, Marguerite, looked uncomfortable, jumped up, and said, "Everyone, this is, um, Marie, our family friend."

I thought to myself, oh hell no, I'm not going to be closeted.

So, I took a deep breath and said, "No, Marie is my partner, not a family friend."

My sister shot me an angry look. There was an awkward silence. Then, at the perfect moment, Mama's best friend and sorority sister, Shirley, sauntered in. She looked stunning as a seventy-seven-year-old Southern lady wearing her black and white tweed suit with pearls, burgundy lipstick, her beautiful silver helmet of thick hair that made her aquamarine eyes pop. Wearing her shiny black pumps and black hose, Shirley was still one classy Southern lady.

I'd known Shirley my whole life and loved her. She and Mama were Tri Deltas at Ole Miss. That's the "Delta, Delta, Delta, can I help ya, help ya, help ya" sorority, class of 1946. I've always loved Shirley because she was the opposite of Mama. She was extroverted, fun, outrageous, and curious, bordering on nosey, in a warm way. Mama was introverted, serious, private, and reserved. Shirley had no filter. She said whatever she thought and felt.

Shirley rushed over to me and gave me a Mama bear hug. God, how I've missed those "squeeze you tight" hugs from older Southern ladies.

"Oh Lizbuth, darling girl, I'm so sorry we lost your Mama! She was my best friend. Well, I hear you brought your partnah. And I don't guess you mean business partnah, do you, darlin'?"

Leave it to Shirley for a fabulous ice breaker at a funeral gathering. Shirley, Marie, and I laughed nervously, while everyone else in the room stared at us.

"Hello, dear Shirley! I'm so glad you're here. This is Marie, my life partner. We've been together for two years."

Shirley smiled, showing her perfectly white teeth, which had to be dentures. Shirley's voice went up an octave, like she was excited and uncomfortable.

"Oh, well, hello, Marie. I'm so glad to meet you, honey."

Shirley looked Marie over from head to toe with that "sizing you up" look that older, coifed, Southern ladies do so well.

"Marie, I'm so glad you and Lizbuth don't wear those big ol' mannish shoes."

Little did Shirley know I had forbidden Marie from wearing her comfortable, big lesbian shoes!

"Lizbuth, darlin, let's go in the kitchen. I have some questions I wanna ask you."

I felt excited and a bit nervous as we made our way back to the kitchen.

"Honey, did your Mama know?"

"Yes, Shirley. Mama knew I'm a lesbian."

"Did she ever meet Marie?"

"No. She refused to meet her. My siblings, Jem and Marguerite only met Marie a few days ago at the hospital in Boston. No one in my family has accepted me, except for a few cousins and my aunts. It's been such a painful journey for me. I never dreamed that Mama would reject me for so long."

"Well, I'm so sorry, Lizbuth. Your Mama was so religious, ever since your brother went off the deep end growing and smoking all that marijuana at Ole Miss back in '65. When we Tri Delta gals traveled together (by the way, we called ourselves "The Golden Girls"), your Mama would bring the Bible, and our friend Annelle would bring the bourbon. Those were wild trips. We called those trips our 'B&B's!'

"Oh, Shirley, I wish I had been with y'all for those trips!"

She grinned and continued, "But listen, darlin, your mother, we called her by her maiden name, Cooper – well, about eight years ago, she stopped talking about you. All of us Golden Girls thought that was the oddest thing. You were her mid-life baby, and she always talked about you. We thought you had cancer or something. Finally, we heard through the Mississippi gossip grapevine about your…situation."

"That I'm a lesbian. Well, what'd you think?"

"Well, I was shocked 'cause you are such a pretty girl, and I knew you'd had boyfriends… But secretly, honey, I was kind of thrilled 'cause I've never known any real live lesbians!"

(I wondered if she knew dead lesbians.)

"Well, Shirley, I'm glad you're kind of excited about it."

We walked back into the living room. Shirley stared at Marie, and then she stared back at me. She walked over to Marie, like she was determined. I held my breath.

"Marie, Sugar, I sure do love that you're a Southern girl from North Carolina! Thank the Lord, Lizbuth didn't end up with a Yankee! That would be more shocking than being gay!" We laughed heartily. Shirley continued to amaze me when she said,

"I want y'all to come visit me down in the Delta this spring. There's nothing like losing your mothah. You know, Cooper and I shared the same birthday, April 16, 1925. And, Marie, I wanna get to know you. Y'all come for Easter, Lizbuth. That will be a hard time for you. We'll share our sadness and our stories about your Mama."

I was thrilled and amazed that Shirley was embracing us.

A few weeks after Mama's funeral, it got difficult for me. My friends stopped calling. Life seemed to go on for everyone around me. My grief descended on me like a thick, gray fog. I didn't sleep or eat well. I couldn't think clearly. I had been orphaned at thirty-nine. Although Marie was supportive of me, she still had her dad. None of my friends had lost both parents. Shirley and I talked on the phone every couple of weeks, which comforted me. She was the only one with whom I could grieve over losing my mother.

Three months later, in April, we flew down to Mississippi again and arrived at Shirley's lovely colonial home on the banks of the bayou in Indianola. Her pink and white azaleas were in full bloom, and her backyard had an explosion of color and new life. I was reminded of the renewing beauty of Mississippi springs. Shirley warmly welcomed us and showed us to our bedroom upstairs. There were twin beds, but she was trying. Then she opened a huge walk-in closet.

"Y'all, these are my favorite evening gowns I wore to the Christmas and debutante balls, at the Country Club. After my awful alcoholic husband, Jewel, dropped dead in the backyard from a heart attack, I decided it was time for me to live! I was only forty-eight, and I started dating fellows as soon as possible–always gentlemen from out of town. There was Bill from Tupelo and David from Jackson... I knew I'd never marry or go to bed with a man again, but once a month or so, I loved having a romantic weekend. My guest bedroom, this room y'all are in, this is where whatever man I dated slept. They've all died, though." Shirley looked wistful and sad for a moment, and then quickly returned to her beaming Southern hostess lady smile.

I looked at Marie and winked. I had a creepy feeling imagining some slightly inebriated, horny old man sleeping in one of the twin beds that Marie or I would be sleeping in.

"You didn't want to marry again, Shirley?" I asked.

"Heavens, no! No more husbands or pets to take care of. I like the freedom I've had for almost thirty years now."

Shirley opened the door to her giant walk-in closet, which had dozens of her evening gowns.

"Y'all see this aquamarine dress? It matches my eyes. People tell me I look like Vivien Leigh. I want to be buried in that one, cuz it props my bosoms up, and makes me look sexy! And I wanna look sexy even when I'm dead."

Marie and I laughed until tears flowed down our cheeks. I was reminded of how much I love this woman. Shirley was certainly a sensual woman in touch with her sexuality, which was so unusual for her generation. Who knows! If she had been born twenty or thirty years later, she could have been bisexual, lesbian, or at least sexually adventurous.

Later that night, Shirley and I stayed up late talking. Marie had gone to bed. Shirley had a burst of her "curious bordering on nosey" attitude.

She said, "Darling, I have a question. I don't quite understand something. You and Marie are both pretty girls, but you are definitely more feminine. So, um... is Marie the man? How does it work?"

I was both tickled and horrified. Shirley wanted to know about our sex life. My God, was she different from my repressed, homophobic Mama!

I recovered quickly from the shock. "Well, Shirley, you know that we Southern ladies do not reveal what goes on behind closed doors. Just use your imagination."

"Oh, honey, I sure will! Tonight, as I'm lying in the bed, I'll be wondering what lesbians do!"

I nearly fell off the couch in hysterical laughter.

We visited Shirley many times over the next ten years and became very close to her. Shortly before our last visit with her, Shirley had had a stroke and was frail, but her spirit was still strong.

On the last night of our visit, Shirley suddenly said, "Y'all, I've been hearing about this gay marriage thing. It's all over the news. And I know y'all got married in San Francisco. I enjoyed looking at your photos. But, Lizbuth, why would y'all wanna do that? Marriage is between a man and a woman."

I took a deep breath. "Shirley, we love each other and wanted to make a commitment to each other. And we want legal rights. Did you know that married heterosexual people have 1,148 federal rights that we don't have?"

"Oh, really? Well, I don't understand it, and I don't think it's Biblical, but I love you girls like you're my own daughters. Y'all are always welcome here. Take care of each other."

"Oh, dear Shirley, we love you, too. Thank you for your stories and laughter and especially for your outrageous questions. You dared to ask questions about my life and my relationship with Marie that Mama never could."

"Don't make me cry. You sweet girls take care of each other. And y'all come back to visit me soon!"

As we drove away, I said to Marie, "I'm so grateful for Shirley. She's helping me heal this motherload of rejection I've been carrying for so long."

About a year later, a few weeks before we were going to visit Shirley in Birmingham, where she had moved to an assisted living center, she died peacefully in her sleep. I was heartbroken. Her funeral was the day before I was performing my first performance of my one-woman play, *A Lesbian Belle Tells*…. I knew I had to attend her funeral, so I rescheduled my show for six weeks later. I performed for a fundraiser for The Mautner Project for women with cancer, a lesbian organization in DC, which went well. After the show, an older man came up to me. I learned that he was a gay Southern psychic from Alabama. You gotta love that!

With a twinkle in his eye, he said, "Hello, Ms. Elizabeth. I'm Steve. Thank you for an outstanding performance. I was truly touched by your stories and your characters. I'd like to ask you a personal question."

"Thank you, Steve. Sure, go ahead."

"Well, are you a spiritual lady? Open to the spirit world? You see, I'm psychic and I have some messages for you."

"Fabulous, Steve! Yes, I'm high woo-woo, and open."

"OK, I saw three lady spirits with you on stage throughout your show. Your Mama, your grandmother, and your mother's friend, Ms. Shirley. They want you to know how proud they are of you, especially Ms. Shirley. She was beaming love at you the whole time."

I had chills. I believed him. And of course, I wanted to hear more.

"Did they say anything more?" I asked.

"They said that you are an amazing storyteller and that they love you very much."

My eyes teared. Steve left me with a final message.

"You know you have psychic gifts, too. They just need to be developed. Meditate more, for at least thirty minutes a day, to raise your spiritual vibration. Your ancestors want to communicate with you more."

Since that evening, I have meditated more. I do feel my ancestors' love for me. I know they are often around me, especially when I perform on stage. I'm open to hearing more from them.

Sadly, in 2003 and 2004, my Mama and all her siblings died. Mama, the next youngest in her family, died first of a stroke in January 2003. Six months later, her younger brother, my Uncle Sonny, died. And six months after that, my Aunt Liber died. A few months later, Aunt Frannie died. In only fourteen months, that whole generation was gone.

I was wracked with grief that year. Losing Mama, of course, was the hardest. Daddy died five years before. Mama and I had so many unresolved issues. My anger, resentment, and regret made it hard to let go. Most of my siblings weren't much help since we had been estranged for so many years. My brother, Reynolds, and his wife reached out and invited Marie and me to their house for Christmas the first year after Mama's death. We went with some hesitation. It was a tender and awkward visit. No one was comfortable expressing grief. I don't think my brother and his family knew any gay people.

My sister-in-law, Karoyl pulled me aside the first night we were there and requested that Marie and I not express affection in front of their children, who were seven and ten.

My response was, "We won't make out in front of them if you and your husband won't." I laughed sarcastically and told her that Marie and I would not be closeted. I suggested that she tell her kids that there are various kinds of couples who love one another–sometimes two women, sometimes two men, and sometimes a man and a woman. Karoyl looked uncomfortable and said nothing.

My grieving process was hard and lonely. I realized that I had needed Mama's acceptance, but we both got stuck in walking circles of disappointment and resentment around each other. We were locked in a power struggle, unable to find understanding and compassion for one another.

Remember, Marie only met my mother when she was on her deathbed, unconscious in a coma. Unfortunately, Mama had refused to meet her for two years. My sister distanced more from me. It hurt that she shut me out of her life even more after Mama died. I felt even more abandoned.

I did everything I could think of to help share, express, and heal my grief. You name the healing modality, and I've probably tried it: grief counseling, bereavement support groups for lesbians, chakra balancing, acupressure, yoga, shamanic breathwork, past life regression, writing classes, visits to psychics and Goddess retreats. And you know what? All of that helped.

As the writer Diane Rooks writes in *Spinning Gold Out of Straw*, "Good stories, particularly ones that deal with loss and healing, can act as vehicles for people to grieve. Stories allow us to acknowledge deep emotions as we become immersed in the story and feel the pain, sadness, despair, and all the other feelings that result from loss. Then healing can begin."

Through spiritual practices like shamanic journeying, shamanic breathwork, and Goddess and Native American rituals and ceremonies, I have reconnected with my parents, aunts, and uncles who have died. I've released and healed most of my abandonment, sorrow, and anger. I feel connected to a Higher Power, a consciousness of love which I prefer to call Spirit, or the Goddess. I've learned that I'm not only a survivor - I'm a thriver. I'm grateful for my own integrity in deciding to come out and live out as a lesbian. Living honestly as who I am is empowering. I have no regrets.

In essence, my Mississippi Mama gave me two precious gifts. She brought me into the world, and I helped her leave. Her death helped bring healing and the renewal of my resilient spirit through surrendering to expressing so much grief.

I've shifted my perspective from seeing my grief as a problem to be solved to realizing that it has been a sacred time in my life, a time in which I have needed and wanted more emotional and spiritual support from people who are closest to me – Marie and a few close friends.

Marie has gradually become more comfortable with my grief, but it has not been easy. As an engineer, she is more comfortable fixing things. Her gifts are analysis, groundedness, and control. She also has a beautiful, compassionate heart. Marie's father died in 2005 from a heart attack. She lost her older brother, Joey, when she was three. Unfortunately, he fell into a pond and drowned going down a culvert at a construction site. This was a tragedy that her family rarely discussed or grieved together. Witnessing my deep grief has opened her to her own.

When Marie and my friends who avoid grief have made suggestions about what I can do to feel better, I have gently told them all I need is to be heard and to receive some loving and kind comments like, "I know this is awful and I can't take away your pain. But I'm here for you, and I love you." I've explained that although this might be hard for them, it is so much more supportive and loving for my feelings of grief, regret, and resentment to be witnessed rather than to receive platitudes and seemingly standard words of comfort.

In his essay, "The Gift of Presence, the Perils of Advice," author Parker Palmer writes, "the human soul doesn't want to be advised or fixed or saved. It simply wants to be witnessed–to be seen, heard, and companioned, exactly as it is. When we make that kind of deep bow to the soul of a suffering person, our respect reinforces the soul's healing resources, the only resources that can help the sufferer make it through."

Although I still sometimes feel sad about the disconnection from my family-of-origin, I also feel gratitude for my struggle. I have forgiven myself and my family for the suffering and separation we have caused ourselves and each other. I define forgiveness as giving up the hope for a better past and living in the present with a sense of peace, compassion, and acceptance. I am no longer a prisoner of my own pain. I believe that my soul chose the perfectly imperfect family to allow me to become the person I am today—a deeply compassionate, loving, and wise woman. I know there is no such thing as overcoming grief. I take comfort in the Buddhist notion of welcoming all my emotions and pushing away nothing. I walk alongside grief and befriend it. Loss and grief are ongoing parts of life. I am fully aware of my own mortality and live my life with intentionality. And I've learned to embrace and express the full range of my emotions from my deepest grief to my highest joy. My heart can hold it all.

CHAPTER 11

Rest My Gay Uncle Sonny's Soul

One of the most unusual Southern funerals in my family was my Uncle Sonny's. He was Mama's younger brother but died only six months after Mama. He'd been living at my Aunt Liber's (his oldest sister's) house in the Mississippi Delta, near Inverness. I'd heard that he'd come for a visit from New Orleans several years back and never left. Apparently, he died in his sleep on Aunt Liber's living room couch. The cleaning lady found him early that morning.

I suspected Uncle Sonny was gay for several reasons. He was secretive about his life and never allowed anyone in his family to visit him in New Orleans. He wouldn't even give anyone his address – only a post office box. He'd married twice briefly and had a daughter by each wife, divorcing each soon after the baby was born. I'd grown up knowing his younger daughter, Lee. She was a year and a half younger than me. I was thrilled to have a cousin close to my age. (Most of my other first cousins were much older than me.) Uncle Sonny's ex-wife, Carolyn, stayed in touch with Mama and Aunt Liber after her divorce. Since Carolyn was an only child and had only one child, we were their only family members, except for Carolyn's mother. I remember going to Aunt Liber's plantation house in the Mississippi Delta for weekends several times a year to see Carolyn and Lee. I loved playing Barbie dolls with Lee and climbing the huge old magnolia tree.

Uncle Sonny only visited us in Okolona once every three or four years. He was my godfather and sent me a birthday card every other year.

Daddy dreaded his visits. He'd say, "Oh hell, Nita, that brother of yours is so damn odd. All he talks about is that Catholic Church and the Communists taking over the world. He's not right. I think he's crazy."

I knew Sonny had been totally estranged from both of his daughters since they were babies, when he divorced each wife. I think his divorces were around nine years apart–one in 1956 and one in 1965. I grew up thinking it was sad and cruel that he refused to meet his daughters. As a child, my cousin, Lee, asked me what her father looked like. She knew he came to visit my parents and me. I remember feeling awkward when she asked me this. I told her he was tall, handsome, and she had his eye shape, but hers were hazel, and his were dark brown. It didn't feel right that Uncle Sonny visited us every few years but had never met his two daughters.

As a teenager, I asked Mama if her brother had some kind of mental illness. I knew he was very strange.

All Mama would say was, "Well, he was in the Korean War and was never the same afterward. The doctor said he was borderline, but as long as he takes his medication, he would be okay." And then she quickly changed the subject.

What did Mama mean "borderline?" Did she mean borderline personality disorder, or borderline mentally ill? She never answered my questions, directly or implicitly.

When I was in graduate school, I took a course in abnormal psychology. As an assignment, I was supposed to interview family members and take a family history of mental illness. I interviewed Mama and Aunt Liber by phone, and my great aunt and uncle, Malva and Red, who lived in Columbia, Maryland, a forty-five-minute drive from my condo in Alexandria, Virginia. Malva and Red were the only civil rights activists in my family. They got run out of their town in McComb, Mississippi by the Ku Klux Klan in 1963. It was quite a story. I digress.

Malva and Red filled me in on my family history. They told me everyone in my mother's hometown knew my Uncle Sonny was very troubled. He was diagnosed as paranoid schizophrenic in his twenties. But apparently, his parents, my grandparents (who had written such passionate love letters to each other in their youth), were ashamed of this and tried to minimize their son's mental illness as "a difficult personality." Thank God for family members who tell the truth.

When my sister-in-law, Karoyl, called to tell me Sonny died, she also told me she and my brother, Reynolds, thought I should call his oldest daughter, Virginia, whom none of my siblings nor I had ever met, and tell her that her father had died. No one wanted that awkward responsibility. Given my passion for people's stories and my interest in meeting my cousin, I took this on. I knew she lived in Clarksdale, Mississippi. I also knew Virginia had searched for her father many times, but he had never responded to her letters. I couldn't imagine that kind of lifelong rejection. And I couldn't imagine the conversation in which I would tell her that her estranged father had died.

I had no idea how to find her. I wasn't sure how much of rural Mississippi was online at this point in 2003. Facebook wasn't a thing yet. The only thing I could think of doing was calling the Chamber of Commerce in Clarksdale. So that's what I did. Here's my memory of that conversation:

"Hello. I have an unusual story. My uncle has recently died, and he was estranged from his daughter. And I think she lives in Clarksdale. His name is Sonny Cooper. Her name is Virginia Smith. Can you help me find her? I've never met her. She needs to know that her dad has died."

"Well, aren't you sweet to do this, darlin? These things happen in families, especially Southern families. When people die, all kinds of stories come spillin' out of the closet... Yes, honey, I know your cousin. Virginia is our dental hygienist at Dr. Clarke's. She's divorced with four kids. And she's such a sweet girl. Here's her cell number, honey. Tell her Annie May gave it to you. Good luck. Bye, now."

All I can say is "only in Mississippi." About fifteen minutes later, I called Virginia. She answered with a raspy voice.

"Hey, Elizabeth, Annie May at the Chamber said you'd be calling. I'm so glad to hear from you. You are Aunt Nita's youngest, right? And your brothers are Jem and Reynolds. Your sister is Marguerite, and she's a year older than me."

I hesitated to break the sad news. I took a big breath and said, "Hello, Virginia. Yes, it's so sad and odd that my siblings and I have never met you. I have some tragic news for you. Your dad died yesterday of a heart attack. He was living at Aunt Liber's house. I'm so very sorry to tell you this."

There was a pregnant pause. Then Virginia's voice quivered, and she began to cry.

"Oh, I'm so heart broken. I never met him. Elizabeth, I can't tell you how many times I wrote to him. I even showed up at his apartment in Slidell one time. No one answered the door. My letters went unanswered. This has haunted me my whole life."

"Oh, Virginia, that's so sad. I'm so sorry. I knew your dad abandoned you and your half-sister, Lee. I grew up knowing her. I'm so sorry I didn't know you. Your dad was, um, mentally ill. I finally got the story about ten years ago from my great Aunt Malva and Uncle Red. He was paranoid schizophrenic. I asked Mama and Aunt Liber about it, but they minimized it and said he was never the same after he returned from the Korean War. Denial has always been a theme in our family."

"Well, I knew something was wrong. Aunt Liber and your mom, Aunt Nita, were very protective of him, I guess."

"I know what it feels like to be rejected by your family. I lost my family when I came out as a lesbian ten years ago. It's a long story."

"Oh, I'm so sorry, Elizabeth. Thank you for telling me that. We have a lot to catch up on."

I was excited to meet a new family member. I imagined we would get to know each other and bond over our family rejection stories. Maybe I could have the kind of older sister I longed for, instead of the estranged sister I had.

Virginia said she would tell her mother and that they might go to the funeral. I encouraged her to go and told her I wanted to meet her and her mother, Betty Anne. I also told her that Sonny's second ex-wife, Carolyn, would probably be there.

"Well, now," Virginia mused. "Won't this be an odd family reunion?"

"Yes, Virginia, it will be a story to remember, for sure."

"Thank you so much for making the effort to call me. This means the world to me."

"You're welcome. I look forward to meeting you."

"Yes, me too, Sweetie. I hope to see you at the funeral home in Indianola."

I flew to Mississippi on a sizzling July morning. Marie couldn't get off work, so I would be attending Sonny's funeral alone.

A few days later, I met Virginia and her mother, Betty Anne. Virginia was around fifty, and her mom was about seventy-two. They looked like proper middle-class Southern ladies, each dressed in a simple black funeral dress, pearls, hose, and black flats. Virginia's eyes were dark, chestnut brown like her father's. She had long, dark hair. She was very warm and friendly. Her mother was a bit more reserved. Betty Anne's eyes were a light, sky blue.

I walked over to them, greeting them each with a big hug. I wanted them to feel welcome.

"Hello, Virginia, and Betty Anne. I'm so glad to finally meet you both. I'm so sorry it is at Sonny's funeral. Come with me, and you can say hello to Aunt Liber. "

Virginia's mother, Betty Anne, took the lead. She suggested we sit down. Then she launched into the story.

"Well, he was mentally ill, Elizabeth. It was so unreal. Sonny would drive to New Orleans to see his men friends. You know he was bisexual or gay. I thought giving him a baby would change things. But he was so paranoid and so angry. And he refused to get psychological help. This was in the 1950s! As soon as Virginia was born, he disappeared, and I demanded a divorce."

Betty Anne definitely knew how to cut to the chase. I admire that in a Southern woman of her generation.

"I'm so sorry. That must have been heart-breaking. And Virginia, for you to not know your father after trying to reach out to him throughout your life. I can't imagine how painful this has been."

I felt a strange sense of guilt. I felt like I needed to apologize on behalf of my uncle, my mother, and Aunt Liber. How could they have rejected these two lovely women? Why did I grow up knowing Carolyn and Lee, but not Betty Anne and Virginia?

Virginia teared up.

"Yes, it's colored my whole life. I married a guy who also abandoned me. That's the story of my life."

Then Betty Anne changed the subject.

"Well, Elizabeth, tell us about your life. Are you married?"

I took a deep breath. Yet another coming out opportunity. The gift that keeps on giving.

"I have a partner, Marie. I'm a lesbian."

Betty Anne took a big gulp of coffee.

"Well, honey, that's okay. It's in your genes. And we still love ya!"

There was an awkward silence. I mean, what could I say to that? "Thank you for still loving me?"

Why did she have to put the word "still" in that sentence?

Then the door of the funeral home opened and in walked Carolyn, my uncle Sonny's second wife. I'd visited with her a few years before, when Marie and I were in the Delta. She was still tall, thin, and elegant, with her white hair, crystal blue eyes, and of course, her black funeral dress, pearls, and black pumps. (Apparently, this was the Southern lady funeral uniform).

This was the first time Sonny's ex-wives had met one another. Carolyn's eyes scanned the room and landed on Betty Anne and Virginia. Carolyn and Betty Anne locked eyes. They seemed to have some awkward bond of sisterly tragedy, each having been married to a violent, mentally ill, bi or gay man.

Then Carolyn broke the awkward silence.

"Betty Anne, dear, I feel like I know your story. Nobody else on this earth understands part of your story the way I do. Bless your heart!"

And then Betty Anne and Carolyn fell into peals of laughter. What else could they do?

There were only about twelve people in the funeral home before the service: my Aunt Liber, who had dementia and wasn't there mentally;

her ex-daughter-in-law, Barbara; Barbara's daughter, my cousin, Marjorie; the Episcopal priest and his wife; and a few church ladies. I think I was the only one to have witnessed the ex-wives meeting.

I encouraged Betty Anne, Virginia, and Carolyn to join us for a family gathering after the funeral. But it was awkward, especially with Aunt Liber's dementia. She was no longer able to be the gracious Southern hostess. I was the last person to stay with Betty Anne and Virginia at the funeral home. Carolyn had left. I wanted to continue our visit, but I think this was all they could handle for one afternoon.

"Let's stay in touch, y'all," I said. I hugged each of these dear women.

"Oh definitely," my cousin Virginia said with a smile.

"Great to meet you, Elizabeth," Betty Anne remarked. "And thank you for helping bring some closure into our lives!"

About a year later, I got a long email from my cousin, Virginia. She wanted to know if there were any possessions her dad had left at Aunt Liber's house. She explained she was looking for medical information for her children's sake. I wrote her back and told her my cousin, Lanny, Aunt Liber's son, was living in her house, and unfortunately, he'd had a stroke and couldn't email. I think I gave her his phone number. I emailed her back and called her, but I never heard back from her. I have thought about Virginia and her mom, Betty Anne, often, and wondered about those relationships that could have developed.

While writing this book, I reached out and reconnected with Carolyn, Uncle Sonny's second former wife, who now lives in an assisted living facility near Memphis, where her daughter, my cousin, lives with her husband and four daughters. We talked for over an hour. We kept up with each other a little on Facebook, but I hadn't seen or talked to her in over four years. She was thrilled to hear from me. Carolyn immediately acknowledged my losses.

"Elizabeth, I'm so sorry that you've lost so many family members and friends. The older you get, the more you'll lose. I've lost so many, too. I'm eighty-two now."

"Oh Carolyn, I'm so sorry you've also lost so many people. Isn't it hard?"

"Yeah, but we're all gonna die, honey. And that's okay. Most of us are going to a good place."

There was a long pause, then Carolyn continued, "I've already donated my body to science, so I'll continue to teach."

Carolyn had been a gifted high school English teacher and a school counselor for many years in the Mississippi Delta. I love that she still had her sense of humor.

Carolyn asked about Marie and her engineering job as she always does. She filled me in on her daughter, Lee, also an engineer, and her four granddaughters.

Then Carolyn started remembering things about being married to my Uncle Sonny. She said he had told her he was schizophrenic and bi-sexual early in their courtship, but she was young and naive and thought she could change him. She also told me he couldn't hold down a job because of his mental illness. She apparently had to whisper in their house because Sonny believed the government was recording their conversations. Unfortunately, he was violent and threatened Carolyn's life several times. I was horrified and saddened hearing her story.

I reminded her about Sonny's funeral. She told me it was a hard decision for her to go to his funeral. I reminded her about meeting Betty Anne and Sonny's oldest daughter, Virginia. I joked with her about the funny and unusual way that she greeted Betty Anne.

And then Carolyn told me something shocking. I was asking her where Virginia was and told her I had tried to contact her years ago when she wanted to know about her dad's belongings and medical records.

"Oh, Virginia died about a year ago," Carolyn told me.

"What? Virginia, Sonny's daughter, died, or do you mean Betty Anne, her mother, died?"

"No, Virginia died."

"What? How did she die? When?"

"I can't remember, honey."

I immediately felt the most unusual kind of loss. I regretted not staying in touch with Virginia after Sonny's funeral. I could have developed a relationship with her. I liked her. She was warm, open, and vulnerable. We probably had similar personalities. Why didn't I stay in touch? Was it too awkward? Was I in such deep grief about Mama's death that I couldn't reach out to her? And what could I do now?

I found her obituary. Virginia died from ALS in October 2017. How I wish someone had contacted me. That damn family estrangement. Here it was again.

I did a little research and found out that her mother, Betty Anne, is still alive and lives in Enid, Mississippi, about ninety miles from my hometown, and she has four grandchildren.

I thought about contacting Betty Anne or even one of Virginia's kids, but what on earth would I say?

Something like, "Hi, I'm Elizabeth, your mom's long-lost first cousin. I met your mom and grandmother once at your estranged, paranoid, schizophrenic, gay grandfather's funeral. He was my Uncle Sonny, my mother's brother. I'm so sorry you lost your mom."

I'm guessing her kids would be in their mid- to late-thirties now. It would be so awkward to try to start relationships with them now. On the other hand, it would be nice to connect with more family.

CHAPTER 12

A Stroke of Grace with Aunt Sue

After Mama and her sisters died, I became close to my Aunt Sue, Daddy's sister, my only living aunt by blood. We talked on the phone at least once a month. Marie and I had visited her several times in Houston. Unfortunately, she had a stroke several years ago, and her health significantly declined. She had been in assisted living facilities, and then a nursing home. Her house has been sold and torn down, and now a soulless McMansion has been built in its place.

About two years after her stroke, I was talking on the phone to her. She asked when Marie and I would be coming to visit her. Out of my mouth popped, "How about Christmas? We could come to see you in Houston."

"Oh, darlin, that would be grand!" she said very slowly in her post-stroke voice.

A few days before Christmas, Marie and I flew to Houston and stayed (at a hotel) for four days to see Aunt Sue and her sons, my cousins, and their families. I felt that Texas Bible belt energy when

I saw the huge billboard that said, "Are you married to Jesus, or are you just dating him on the weekends?" You can't make this shit up! I must admit, though, that sign was a creative marketing strategy from some Baptist church.

Marie and I had visited Aunt Sue many times over the years, but this was the first time we'd visited her since she moved into an assisted living facility. I was shocked to see how much she had declined. She looked frail, old, and vulnerable. She could barely talk. I think she had developed dementia. She had always been so kind to Marie and me. Ever the extrovert and engaging conversationalist, now Aunt Sue had no filter. We ate dinner with her in her dining room at the assisted living center, where most people were much higher functioning. Her nursing aid wheeled her into the dining hall and left us alone for a visit. Suddenly Aunt Sue frowned at me and scolded, "Elizabeth, stop staring at the ladies here. I see you looking them over from head to toe. You still look at ladies' shoes."

Was she having a homophobic moment, or was she annoyed that I was paying attention to the other old ladies there? Who knows? I replied in a light-hearted way, "Oh, you know how I love shoes! I have been fascinated with them since I was a little girl."

Aunt Sue said nothing. It was taking her forever to eat her dinner. I was getting impatient with her. Marie and I had long finished our meal. Marie asked her questions and tried to engage her in conversation, but it seemed to take all of Aunt Sue's concentration to get the food on her fork and into her mouth. A lot of the food was dropping onto her chest. It was heartbreaking to watch this. This was not my glamorous, vivacious, talkative Aunt Sue. Where did she go? What happened to her brain? That damn stroke and dementia had hijacked her. And I would never get my dear Aunt Sue back. It felt like her soul was gone. All that remained was a cranky old woman who behaved like a toddler.

Aunt Sue looked exactly like her mother, my grandmother, in her 80s. I saw the same arthritic hands and the same gray helmet hairdo.

No matter how hard I tried, I couldn't stop my feelings of disappointment. I couldn't be present with her. Gone was my natural ability for compassion and empathy. Gone were the mindfulness skills I'd cultivated in those meditation groups I'd been in for so many years.

I took deep breaths, noticing the mix of my intense emotions – frustration, shock, sorrow, and disappointment. The Buddhist mantra played in my head, "Welcome everything. Push away nothing." Yeah, well, today was not a Buddhist kind of day.

Then I noticed a few familiar things about Aunt Sue–her scarlet nails that matched her sweater. I noticed and felt my tears well up when I watched her struggle to sign her meal ticket. The only way she knew to be my aunt was to pay for our meal. I was touched and so sad.

Marie and I went back to Aunt Sue's apartment that evening. We listened to her animated singing Christmas tree with eyeballs and a mouth that popped open. I fondly remembered how much Aunt Sue loved to decorate for Christmas. This odd-looking Christmas tree reminded me of her playful, childlike spirit. Together, we sang:

We wish you a Merry Christmas,
We wish you a Merry Christmas,
We wish you a Merry Christmas,
and a Happy New Year!

Then we looked at her scrapbooks from her senior high school prom and her college years at Ole Miss from 1943-1947. There was an old, dried rose from her high school prom in the scrapbook. I noticed it had an old, faintly sweet scent. I showed it to Aunt Sue. Suddenly she lit up and began to remember her high school dates' names, "Billy, John, and David." She mentioned something about a speech she gave at her graduation in 1941. How I wish she had a copy of that, and a YouTube video!

We were all present and connected to one another while we looked at her memorabilia from so long ago. Somehow, I made a shift from being impatient to being in the moment. I opened my heart to gratitude for Aunt Sue. I marveled at the history she lived. Finally, I could be present with her in our connections to our Southern stories. I realized this was the intention I wanted to set for the new year.

Our visit with Aunt Sue taught me about the importance of paying attention and slowing down to match her slowing rhythm in the winter of her life. I was grateful for my grief, my joy, and even my impatience with Aunt Sue.

As I was writing this book, my dear Aunt Sue died peacefully on a Sunday morning. Another huge loss for everyone in my family. She was the last one of my parents' generation. She was quite the Southern belle and steel magnolia. I miss Aunt Sue's stories and her sense of style. I feel fortunate to have had a close bond with her. Now, I realize that I am part of the "older generation," which is shocking. I can only hope that I am aging with grace and style that would make Aunt Sue proud.

CHAPTER 13

You Can Go Home Again

The year I turned fifty was a rite-of-passage into a new chapter of my life. I'd made peace with so many difficult passages in my life– my parents' deaths, the challenges of menopause, and my estrangements from my siblings - and yet, I was feeling a kind of homesickness for my motherland down in northeast Mississippi in Chickasaw County. Even with the pain of my family story, I still value my ties to the Deep South. There is a tribal bond I feel with other Mississippians. I appreciate and struggle with eccentric small-town culture– everybody knowing everybody's business, the friendliness of people who have had ties to one's family members for many years, the willingness to help one another in times of need–especially during illness and death. I hate the prejudice towards anyone who is not heterosexual, white, Southern, and Protestant Christian. I struggle with the racism, sexism, and homophobia. As I mentioned before, I love our rich tradition of Southern writers, storytellers, and blues music. Mississippi is an odd mix of paradoxes that I find fascinating and frustrating. Writer Richard Grant describes my home state well in his book, *Dispatches from Pluto.* He writes:

"Outsiders often see it as a paradox that such a poor, conservative, religious state should also have such a rich literary tradition, but it makes sense to Mississippians. Not only are they great tellers and admirers of colorful stories, with a rich supply of material; there's also an intangible, mysterious quality to life here that Mississippi writers have felt compelled to tackle, a kind of magical realism that comes out of the state's long insularity."

I was keenly aware that only a few people were still living from my parents' generation. Some of my favorites were Bob and Emily Henson, who had traveled with my parents when I was a teenager. I called them my parents' "younger, cooler, atheist friends." They'd known my parents since 1950 and had been in the weekly "Supper Club" with them, as well as had adventures on international trips together. (They were the talk of the town when they went to India and Afghanistan in 1979.)

Bob was a successful business owner, a board member at the Bank of Okolona, and about twelve years younger than my father. As a child, I remember him as being fun, positive, and encouraging. Daddy was depressed, negative, and skeptical. I grew up longing for Bob to be my father.

Emily was nine years younger than my mother. She was very intelligent and loved to read mystery novels. I admired her gourmet cooking skills, her neat, beautiful home, and her perfectly manicured, cantaloupe-colored nails. Mama only read Christian books and was not domestically skilled. She never wore nail polish.

It had been several years since I'd been to my hometown to visit. Somehow, I talked Marie into driving down to Okolona to spend most of Thanksgiving week. We stayed in a cute cottage out in the country on a beautiful property owned by my parents' younger friend, Mike. In the midst of rolling hills of Monroe County in northeast Mississippi, there were two guest cottages, a lake with swans, a meditation space, and plenty of Buddhas and Kuan Yins from his travels to China. Mike is the kind of introvert who builds guest cottages for his friends to visit him.

Bob and Emily's farm, called Hayfield Farm, a few miles outside of Okolona, had a swimming pool and tennis courts. As a teenager visiting home from boarding school and college in the summers, I spent many lazy August afternoons sunning, reading, and swimming at their pool. When the heat was unbearable, I'd go into the house and sit with Emily at the kitchen counter, sipping iced tea and smoking cigarettes. I would often complain about how overly religious Mama was.

On one such occasion, Emily paused, took a slow intense drag from her Virginia Slim cigarette, and said, "Well, yes, your mother went overboard with the religion thing when your brother, Jem got into drugs at Ole Miss. I like Nita, but we're very different, and we have an agreement that we avoid the topics of religion and politics. She's married to Jesus, the Episcopal Church, and your dad. Bob and I quit going to that Presbyterian Church. I prefer Buddhist philosophy and dogs, which are much more interesting than religion."

I appreciated how Emily validated my frustrations with Mama. Years later, I called Emily and came out to her. I told her Mama and Daddy had rejected me.

She said, "I have no problem with your lifestyle. But what do you want me to do, Elizabeth?"

Emily was not a touchy, feely type. She was a doer, a fix-it kind of woman. I'm guessing she was worried I wanted her to pressure Mama to accept me.

"I don't need you to do anything, Emily. I wanted you to know. I thought you would be accepting."

"Absolutely, Elizabeth. I'm sorry your parents are giving you a hard time. I don't think they'll change. But you're always welcome here."

Years later, after my parents died, Marie and I started visiting Bob and Emily. They both loved Marie. Bob and Marie had engineering degrees and a love for gardening. Emily and Marie both loved reading Tom Clancy novels. I sometimes wondered if they enjoyed Marie more than me. In fact, the last time we visited them, Emily whispered to Marie, "I wish you were my daughter." Bob realized that I heard this comment and hugged both Marie and me, as he declared, "you girls are our daughters." I will never forget that moment. I always felt Bob's loving father-like energy.

Bob pulled me into the conversation by telling stories about my parents from their younger days.

"Honey, did I tell you about the time at our Supper Club when your Mama shocked everybody?"

I'd heard this story a dozen times, but never tired of hearing Bob tell it in his animated, loving, extroverted way, "Well, your Daddy tried to control your Mama. One night, he told her not to smoke and to stop drinking for the night. She disappeared from the room, and, in a few minutes, she pranced through the room with a lit cigarette in both ears, both nostrils, two in her mouth and holding a gin and tonic in her hands. And she held her head high and didn't say a word."

We'd all howl with laughter after these stories. I felt connected to my parents through their friends, Bob and Emily. Oh, the power of their stories.

While Marie and I were lounging in Mike's guest cottage on Thanksgiving morning, Bob called to say that Emily had too much back pain, and they weren't feeling well enough to have us over that afternoon. I was disappointed. (Little did I know that Emily and Bob's health was on a swift decline and that in less than two years they would be gone.)

There weren't many restaurants open on Thanksgiving in rural Mississippi, where everyone was expected to be home with their families. We didn't have much food in the cottage either. Where would we go? I imagined us in some country restaurant with cooked to death food that would clog our arteries. Yuck.

We found one restaurant open that was still taking reservations, Woody's in Tupelo, twenty-five miles up the road. When we got there, I remembered this was the restaurant I went to on one of my last dates with an old boyfriend, Stacy, thirty years ago. He died tragically in a motorcycle accident five years before this Thanksgiving event.

I unexpectedly had what I call a "grief ambush" while we were eating at this restaurant. Suddenly, I was flooded with memories of dates with Stacy. The last date we had was at this very restaurant on New Year's Eve twenty-one years earlier, which was the year before I came out. I couldn't stop crying. I had to go to the restroom several times to tend to my tears. Poor Marie. I was definitely not good company that day.

As we drove back to the cottage, I called a friend of Mama's, Sandra, who was a retired Presbyterian minister. I hadn't seen her in over thirty years. For some reason, I felt a longing to visit her. We drove right past her house on the way back to Mike's cottage.

Sandra had been the first of the two female ministers in my hometown. She was called to the First Presbyterian Church in 1986. Mama and I once visited her and went to a service to hear her preach. Our first visit with her, Sandra told us she'd had a daughter who tragically died in a car accident when she was only sixteen. Her name was Elizabeth, and she would have been my age. I felt a connection to Sandra when she told us this.

A few months before our trip down South, I had read in my hometown newspaper, the *Okolona Messenger*, that Sandra's husband had died. I called her, and we reconnected. I told her that Marie and I were coming to Mississippi for a visit. She was excited and said she wanted us to come to her house to see her. I had already come out to her in a phone conversation a few months before that. She was very supportive. I told her how my family had rejected me.

She said, "Oh darlin, I wish you had told me years ago. Maybe I could have helped your mother accept you."

I was deeply touched and grateful that she was so accepting. I regretted not calling Sandra twenty years before to get her support, but I had been too afraid of more rejection and condemnation.

Marie and I found time to go to Sandra's on our way back from that sad Thanksgiving dinner.

We arrived at Sandra's large colonial home nestled in an orchard of live oak trees. She was etched in my memory as a trim, forty-five-year-old, blonde-haired woman from the 1980s. When she opened the door and greeted us, an older, rounder, gray-haired woman in her seventies was standing before us in a Kelly-green, Santa-sporting, velour sweat suit and goldish-green bedroom slippers. Aging has its way with us all, I guess.

Sandra welcomed us warmly. She threw her arms around me and said, "Oh, my dear Elizabeth. I'm so glad to see you again. And Marie, I can't wait to get to know you because you belong to Elizabeth. Y'all come on in."

Sandra had a passion for the color green. Everything was in varying shades of green. We had "pink wine" as she called it, in green wine glasses. The carpet throughout her house was forest green. And her living room couch was deep bell pepper green.

Sandra was engaging and friendly. She asked all about our life together in Washington and asked about Marie's job. She talked about how much she had loved my mother. And she shared about how hard it was to be the first female minister in town in the 1980s.

"I could feel the sexism in that congregation every time I stood at that pulpit to preach. It only took 'em six months to decide they liked having a woman minister. Then once I buried and married a few folks, I was in their hearts as their minister."

The next morning, I went back to Sandra's house to have a one-on-one visit with her. I knew Marie needed some alone time, and I wanted a longer visit with Sandra.

Having tea with Sandra in her lime green kitchen, which hadn't been renovated since the 1970s, I felt a sense of connection and comfort. I seem to be drawn to older Southern women. Sandra was no Shirley, Mama's outrageous sorority sister. She was younger than Shirley but not as flamboyant. She confided to me about her struggles with grief and depression after her daughter died in 1983. On a tour of her house, she paused in the hallway on our way to her bedroom.

Sandra said, "Look, here are photos of my Elizabeth on her horse."

Her voice shifted to a more tender, vulnerable tone.

"Oh, how lovely," I said. "How old would she be if she were alive today?"

"Honey, she would have turned fifty earlier this month."

"Oh, wow, Sandra, my fiftieth birthday was a few weeks ago. When was your Elizabeth's?"

"It was on the eighth."

"Oh, my God!"

We exchanged a look of profound connection and knowing.

"Elizabeth, is that your birthday, too?"

"It certainly is."

We paused and looked deeply into one another's eyes to take in this strange and miraculous connection.

Sandra then burst into tears and fell into my arms.

"Oh, this is a God thing, darlin. We are supposed to be in each other's lives to help each other."

"Wow, Sandra… yes. I'm so grateful that we've reconnected. I trusted my intuition that I was supposed to visit you."

Sandra told me how awful it was to lose her only daughter. Her grief had turned into depression. I shared about how hard it was to lose Mama after I came out and how complicated my grieving process was.

"Well, honey, I'm so sorry. I totally accept and love you. This is how God made you. And I love Marie. I can see that y'all are soulmates."

I filled Marie in on all of this when I returned to our cottage.

"Wow, Elizabeth, that's incredible. Y'all were supposed to reconnect and share your stories. Now you have another Southern Mama."

On our drive back to Maryland the next day, Sandra called me.

"Darlin, I still can't get over our connection. I'm so glad you're back in my life. I'll be your earthly mother, and you can be my earthly daughter. And we can heal each other's hearts."

I reflected on the pattern of endings and beginnings with Shirley's death, Emily and Bob's declining health, and reconnecting with Sandra. Where one chapter ends, another one begins. I was filled with gratitude, for I knew that my Mississippi connections still mattered. Intuitively, I knew that my reconnection with Sandra was some kind of Divine intervention. Our journeys through grief–her loss of her daughter, also named Elizabeth, who was born on my birthday, November 8, 1963, and the loss of my mother deepened our friendship. And I knew that I could indeed go home again.

CHAPTER 14

Friendship and Forgiveness

I've been blessed with some extraordinary lesbian friendships in my life. My friendship with a woman named Marti had to be the most intense and unusual friendship I've ever had, filled with joy and frustration. Thirteen years my senior, she was louder, stormier, more outrageous, and extroverted than I. While we were both intense feminists who loved to laugh and process feelings, there were striking differences in our personalities and backgrounds. Marti was extremely anxious, and I was relatively calm. She came out in New York City in 1976 after a short-lived marriage to a man. I came out in Washington, DC in 1994 and never married a man. Marti grew up in a wealthy, liberal, New England family. I grew up in a wealthy, conservative, Southern family. In many ways, Marti was the ideal lesbian sister I'd always wanted. We were both psychotherapists in Asheville. I met her soon after the summer Marie and I moved to those beautiful Blue Ridge Mountains from Washington, DC Marti took me under her wing by helping me find office space and introducing me to other therapists and to her friends.

A lively Leo, Marti could tell the funniest stories for hours on end. She educated me about the history and meaning of butch/femme relationships and lesbian feminist politics. Marti could also be vulnerable and raw in telling me about her traumatic childhood, her coming out process, and how she got sober through joining Alcoholics Anonymous. We would laugh hysterically together one day, and a few days later, Marti would get mad at me for something I thought was minor. She'd storm out of a restaurant in a rage. It was the most volatile friendship I ever had. I never knew what kind of mood Marti would be in. I soon discovered that she had been diagnosed as bipolar, which is a serious mood disorder. Unfortunately, Marti stopped taking her medication. When she had a manic episode, she'd see thirty clients in three days and clean out all her closets. She attributed this to being a fast-paced, neurotic, New Yorker.

I loved hearing her stories of being an activist in the feminist movement in New York, where she planned and attended dozens of dyke marches in the gay pride parades. I'd read about lesbians like Marti, who went to consciousness-raising feminist book groups, and Goddess retreats where they howled at the moon and examined their vaginas with hand mirrors. Tears from outrageous laughter rolled down my cheeks when I heard these stories.

Marti could also be a good listener. We'd moved to Asheville only a year and a half after Mama died. Having descended into the underworld of grief and depression, I was climbing out of the darkness. Daddy had died six years before. My journey through orphanhood was still complicated by my estrangement from my siblings. Marti had also lost both of her parents and was estranged from her two brothers. She supported me through my grief that year. She reminded me of how important it was to laugh in the midst of loss.

Marti also helped me understand the paradox of this little, funky, mountain town, Asheville. One day, I was complaining to her about how small and Southern it felt. I had read that it was a small, progressive city with 40,000 lesbians. (Some article online written by a lesbian made this ridiculous claim.) I'm guessing at the time (in 2004), there were under 1,000 lesbians living in the Asheville area. We saw the same 20 women at every lesbian social event.

I was having some regret that I gave up city life and my private practice in the Washington, DC area. I had pressured Marie to move with me. In fact, I moved to Asheville first and had a rough landing–including having the moving company take twenty-two days to arrive with my belongings. I didn't know anyone. Three months later, Marie arrived with no job. We were both feeling lost and wondering what we'd gotten ourselves into.

I noticed the lesbian community in Asheville was very small. There was less diversity, and Asheville lesbians were more interested in biking, hiking, and fishing. DC lesbians were more interested in politics, theater, museums, and dinner parties. When I shared these differences with Marti, she chuckled and said, "I know exactly what you mean, girl. How do you think I felt coming from New York City fifteen years ago?"

As it turned out, we only lived in Asheville for three years from 2004 to 2007. Although we loved those beautiful mountains and made some great friends, we missed the big city life of Washington, DC, with its cultural diversity, huge Pride events, museums, and great theaters. Marie wanted a more challenging and better paying job. Eventually, she decided to apply for a federal job in DC so she could have a pension. I knew I could start a private practice again. Marie and I especially missed singing in the Lesbian and Gay Chorus of Washington. So, we decided to move back.

When I told Marti we were moving back to DC, she immediately got angry and withdrew from our friendship. I believe she felt abandoned. I remember her storming out of a café where we were having breakfast. I was stunned. Over the next several months, I called Marti to try to reconnect. I even wrote her a card of gratitude before we moved and told her how much her friendship meant to me. I had hoped to reconnect with her. I heard nothing but her silence. That summer (2007), we moved back to the DC area. I was glad to be back, but I missed Marti, other friends, and those mystical mountains.

Five years later, I was visiting Asheville, attending a storytelling workshop. Somehow Marti's name came up because Asheville is a small town and someone in the workshop knew her. This woman told me Marti had been recently diagnosed with stage four pancreatic cancer. I learned that she had already closed her private practice and had given herself a living wake to say goodbye to her friends and celebrate her life. This was so Marti! I thought that was a very bold move. I admired her courage.

I was shocked and so sad. I hesitated about whether to contact her, since our friendship had ended so abruptly five years before. Could I risk being rejected again? Would Marti want to reconnect with me at the end of her life? I knew that pancreatic cancer is awful and takes people out fast. I decided to call her and have no expectations about whether she would return my call or not.

I called her and left a rambling heartfelt message that went something like this:

"Hi, Marti. This is Elizabeth McCain, a blast from the past. I'm in Asheville for a few days. I'm so sorry about your health situation. Please know you are in my thoughts and prayers. I know we haven't been in each other's lives for the past several years, but I would welcome the opportunity to talk to you. And if you're not up for that, I'll understand. I have missed our friendship, Marti. You're in my heart. I send you peace and love. Take care."

I hung up and felt a combined sense of sorrow and peace. While I tried not to have expectations, I had a glimmer of hope that Marti would call me. If she did, what would she say? What would I say? Would I ever see her again or hear her hearty laughter again? Would I find out why she abruptly disappeared from my life? Would I want to know? Would we make amends? I knew since she was facing her death, and since we were only friends for a couple of years, there was only a slim chance that she would return my call.

To my delight, Marti returned my call the next day while I was at my workshop.

"Hi, Elizabeth. It's Marti. I'm so glad you called! I've been thinking about you and how stupid I was to hold on to resentment towards you. I'd love to talk to you and maybe have a visit over tea. Call me tonight. If we don't catch up over the next few days, would you come back to Asheville to visit me soon? This is quite a journey I'm on, and I have so much to tell you. This cancer shit is a fucking nightmare and one hell of a way to have a wake-up call in my life at sixty-two. Lots of love to you!"

We talked for a long time later that night – our usual familiar combination of deep sharing, laughter, and tears. In some ways, it felt like we picked up where we left off five years before.

Marti was filled with regrets, as she said, "Oh, Elizabeth, I'm so glad we're talking. I've thought a lot about you since I was diagnosed with this awful cancer a few months ago. I was thinking of writing you a letter and making amends with you. I remember you reached out to me several times before y'all moved back to DC. I was stupidly holding onto a lot of resentment toward you. I have so many regrets about so many things in my life. Here I am facing death in a short while. Letting our friendship die was one of my biggest mistakes. I'm so sorry, Elizabeth."

I took a deep breath and said, "It's okay, Marti. Thank you for your apology. I've missed you, too. I'm so sorry you're sick. What's important is that we're connecting now."

"Yeah, you're right. You know why our personalities sometimes clashed? I think it was because we're so alike! You know, we're both intense and emotional drama queens–with all our abandonment shit from childhood–mother loads of it, right? God, we're so alike!"

Actually, I was shocked to hear her say that. While we were both emotional, I was more mindful of my expression of emotions in public and have never ended a friendship out of momentary frustration. Of course, I kept these opinions to myself. I wanted to support Marti in this last chapter of her life. I was able to let go of my judgments about her and focus on what I loved about her. I loved her intellectual curiosity. I loved her stories about being part of the dyke marches in New York's Pride parades. I loved her extroverted nature. I loved the twinkle in her bright blue eyes when she told a bawdy joke. I loved her ability to be vulnerable. I loved that she had been sober for over thirty years and was a sponsor and mentor for so many recovering alcoholics. Most of all, I loved the sound of Marti's laugh–a hearty, deep laugh that filled the room.

Marti asked me to visit her that June and support her through her life review process. I agreed and felt honored that she trusted me to hear her deepest regrets and accomplishments. So, six weeks later, I returned to Asheville. Although Marti was glad she helped so many clients get sober, she realized she spent too much of her life working and worrying. I was saddened to hear her say, "Damn, I got it all wrong. I focused too much on work. And I failed at love." (Marti was single for the last ten years of her life. She had only a couple of long-term relationships.) Hearing her review her life was intimate and poignant. And it was a wake-up call for me to let go of my own regrets and live my life fully.

I'm sure Marti's constant stress and anxiety fueled her work addiction and contributed to her illness. In the last two years of her life, she worked as a therapist at a women's prison. With the collapse of the economy in 2007, she needed a full-time job. Marti told me it was the most stressful job she'd ever had with endless paperwork, difficult personalities, conflict among the staff, and clients who were serious drug addicts with no motivation or hope. She said a few months before her digestive problems started (symptoms of the pancreatic cancer) she had been saying out loud, "This job is killing me."

It was hard for me to witness her regret and grief. Marti didn't want to die. She was in agonizing pain for the last couple of months. It was an honor to hear her stories. Rather than trying to take her pain away, I listened, gave her empathy, and hugs. When she asked me if I believed in heaven, I said, "I'm sure there is some kind of afterlife. And I am confident that you will be there surrounded by your parents and other loved ones."

Marti was estranged from one of her brothers for many years. She wrestled with the concept of forgiveness and wanted to know if I thought she should forgive him. I encouraged her to make the right decision about that from her soul, rather than her ego. And I shared my favorite definition of forgiveness from *A Course in Miracles*, "forgiveness is giving up all hope for a better past." I also told her that forgiveness is about letting go of suffering, blame, and old stories that no longer serve us. We agreed we could forgive people without having reconciliation. Then she folded her arms and declared, "But there's still a part of me that wants that motherfucker shit of a brother to apologize to me." And we howled with laughter.

On the last day of my visit, I was deeply touched when Marti gave me a quilt she made from all the t-shirts she had worn at gay pride marches in New York from 1975 to 1990. As we cried together, Marti said, "Elizabeth, you gotta carry the torch now as the next generation behind me. The world needs your boldness, your irreverence, and of course, your stories. Finish writing your one-woman play and share it with the world!"

In fact, on the last night of my visit, Marti hosted a small gathering of her friends and invited me to share the coming out stories I was writing for my one-woman play. I was so touched that she was still supporting me in her last chapter of life. That night, we all laughed and cried together. There was an unspoken knowledge that this was our last social gathering with Marti, which made it especially poignant.

A couple of months later, on August 31, a few weeks after her sixty-second birthday, I received a phone call from a friend of Marti's telling me she had died. I felt the shock and deep sadness about never seeing her again. I also felt joy and a sense of relief that Marti was no longer suffering. As a kind of ritual, I called Marti's cell phone sobbing and told her how much I would miss her and thanked her for our friendship. I invited her to visit me in my dreams. That night there was a blue moon. I dreamed that Marti came to me, and said, "Well, of course you called my cell phone and left a long, emotional message! We loved to talk on the phone and leave each other long voicemail messages. That was our thing! Oh, Elizabeth, you were a once in a blue moon kind of friend. I love ya, girl. Gotta go now."

I'm incredibly grateful for my reconciliation and reconnection with my friend, Marti. I felt honored that she asked me to witness her life review. I was equally awed when she included me in a meeting with her friends to help her plan her memorial service.

I missed Marti so much after she died. Since we no longer lived in Asheville, I had no community with whom I could share my grief. Marti's death taught me how to be with my grief. Instead of overcoming or avoiding it, I learned to welcome my grief and grow through it. When we love people, we always risk losing them. Eventually, we will lose everyone and everything. Grief is simply the price we pay for loving.

CHAPTER 15

From the Story to the Stage

One of the most transformative activities I've done to heal my grief has been sharing my stories with people. Whether I am on a porch, at a dinner table, or on a stage, sharing stories in a community is one of my greatest passions. I believe that story is the soul's medicine for healing just about everything.

Having grown up in rural Mississippi, where everyone knew everybody's business, I'd always been captivated listening to my family members and friends share their personal stories. This is how we learned how to connect with people, know one another, and be known. As I've mentioned before, we Mississippians have a rich story tradition in Southern literature and blues music. I hail from a long ancestral line of eccentric storytellers in Mississippi, Tennessee, North Carolina, and Virginia. My older ancestors were from England, Wales, Scotland, and Ireland, countries rich in Celtic legend and story. So, it's in my blood, my very own DNA.

In 2006, I discovered storytelling as an art form at a storytelling workshop from an internationally known storyteller, Connie Regan-

Blake, when Marie and I lived in Asheville, NC. When we moved back to the Washington, DC area in 2007, we missed being around other Southerners. I remember talking to our gay Southern friend, Bill, about how much I loved going to the National Storytelling Festival, which Marie and I had attended the year before. Bill told me about a storytelling organization in DC, called Speakeasy DC (now Story District). I went to one of their storytelling shows and was mesmerized. People got up on the stage and told a seven-minute personal story. There was a feeling of universal connection in the audience as we listened to the storytellers. Soon, I took a storytelling class and was hooked. I fell even more in love with the craft of storytelling, something I'd been doing naturally with my family and friends my entire life. I noticed that when we had parties at our house, people loved to sit around the fireplace and tell stories. The feeling shifted in the room. Everyone listened with rapt attention. There was a magical energy that everyone felt.

In 2010, I thought I might have enough stories to write and perform my own one-woman play. I took solo performance classes and received theater and story coaching. I hired a theater director to coach me through writing my own solo show. I remembered the promise I'd made to my friend Marti to finish writing my play. I fulfilled that promise when I first performed *A Lesbian Belle Tells...* in 2013 for a fundraiser for the Mautner Project for lesbians with cancer. The next year, I performed an improved and expanded version of my play in the 2014 Capital Fringe Theater Festival, where it was voted best solo show from DC Broadway World. Writing and performing my play was emotionally cathartic and healing for me because it is about my true stories of growing up in Mississippi, coming out in DC in the 90s, experiencing family estrangement, and finding love and belonging. As told from the comfort of my rocking chair, my show has captivating moments of Southern gothic comedy, as well as triumph over tragedy, as only a lesbian belle can tell.

It's been an honor to have performed my play and shorter stories in DC, Baltimore, Rehoboth Beach, Asheville, Tennesee, Mexico, Ireland, Fringe Festivals, Pride Festivals, and at government agencies, house concerts, universities, and spiritual retreats. As of this writing, my play recently got booked for Oxford Pride, where the University of Mississippi, "Ole Miss" is located. Almost everyone in my family graduated from this university, including my parents, and my brother Reynolds, who received his bachelor's and medical degrees from there. My maternal grandfather, Pop, received his law degree from Ole Miss around 1920. The Deep South has come a long way. Thanks to the younger generations of students and professors, there is now a vibrant LGBTQ and allies' community in Oxford, which is nothing short of amazing. I'm so grateful to have opportunities to perform in the Deep South. Now my story about my homeland in Mississippi has transformed from one of rejection to one of celebration.

At first, it was terrifying performing my play. I was afraid that homophobic, religious, right-wing people might come out to harass me–especially after Trump was elected. It was painful to revisit my loss, grief, and family estrangement complications. I committed myself to doing more of my inner work through energy healing, acupressure, grief counseling, and writing workshops and retreats. Each time I rehearsed, and each time I stepped onto the stage, I felt like I was owning my power and reclaiming my story. It got easier. I loved having audience members speak to me after my performance. All ages, sexual orientations, and gender identities of people have wanted to share their stories of loss and coming out. I began to lead workshops on the power of LGBTQ+ stories and healing grief through story. Sometimes people started working with me privately in counseling and story coaching sessions.

I knew I had discovered more of my soul purpose in supporting and inspiring LGBTQ+ communities, and our allies in sharing and reframing their stories for their own personal growth transformation, and community building. My gift of sharing and witnessing stories had been inside me all along. It took me a while to realize this.

Through performing, I've also deepened friendships in the storytelling community. This helped me step out of social isolation and into life. I've learned to own and appreciate my extroverted nature and open heart. I approach my life as an incredible adventure, knowing that another great story can be happening either in the present moment or right around the corner.

CHAPTER 16

My First Lesbian Cruise on Olivia

In 2013, Marie and I realized we no longer had a lesbian community anywhere. The Washington, DC LGBTQ health clinic, Whitman-Walker Clinic, had closed their lesbian services department and fired several lesbian staff members about five years before. That same year, the Lesbian and Gay Chorus of Washington also dissolved. When the DC LGBTQ Community Center finally opened, the word "lesbian" didn't appear anywhere on their website. The only support groups were for retired gay men, trans people, queer, and non-binary people. I didn't understand why spaces for lesbians were disappearing.

Several of our lesbian friends had kids or were busy caregiving for their elderly parents. Others relocated. We saw them less and less. We had some friendships with single, straight women and a gay male couple, but I needed more than that. I craved deeper friendships with other like-minded lesbians. In 2010, I joined the

New Wave Singers, the LGBTQ+ chorus in Baltimore, which was forty-two miles away. I befriended some lesbian sopranos. To my delight, I gathered with several of these women for dinner every Tuesday before our rehearsal. But, unfortunately, Marie couldn't sing in New Wave with me because of her work schedule. We were not sharing a lesbian community, which saddened me. We lost interest in going to Capitol Pride because we no longer saw our lesbian friends. We thought that Capitol Pride in DC was too hot, too large, and too corporate. Marie and I realized that we were becoming isolated from lesbian culture, which saddened us. It was hard feeling like we were the only lesbians our age in the DC area. Where were our sisters?

Along came my fiftieth birthday. Despite this bleak social backdrop, Marie asked me what I wanted to do to celebrate. Two possibilities came to mind: a high-end Olivia lesbian cruise to the Virgin Islands, or a Goddess trip to Ireland or Greece. Together we decided that, given our desire for lesbian community, we would go on an Olivia cruise. We chose the New Year's trip to the Virgin Islands because of the entertainment, which included eighty-four-year old marriage equality activist Edie Windsor, Chris Williamson, and Billie Jean King. The trip was over New Year's, and we thought a lesbian cruise on Olivia would be the perfect way to start 2014. Edie Windsor's case had won on the Supreme Court, which was about to make gay marriage legal throughout the country.

I was thrilled to be on this lesbian cruise. My forties had been hell, filled with the heaviness of grief from my mother's and my aunts' deaths and the deaths of several friends. I was determined that my fifties would be much better. Marie and I set our intentions to meet cultured, interesting, fun, spiritual lesbians on the Olivia cruise.

Ours was a smaller ship. Only three hundred lesbians. THREE HUNDRED LESBIANS?! I was in heaven. I looked around at the community of sisters we would adventure with for the next six days and immediately felt my anxiety rising about fitting into this lesbian culture and finding our tribe with lesbian couples.

My belonging issues came back to haunt me. Suddenly, I felt like I was fourteen again. I still struggled with fitting into lesbian culture. I didn't and still do not have a "lesbian look." I'm not butch, athletic, sporty, nor am I the hippy-dippy looking kind of lesbian. As I've described before, I'm a mainstream-looking femme—a "lipstick lesbian." Where were other lesbians who looked like me? In one corner were the glamorous Texas lesbians from Dallas and Houston wearing tight jeans, cowboy hats, lots of heavy eye make-up, and big, frosted hair. In another corner were the tan, butch lesbians from Arizona and Southern California, who looked like they spend their days on a golf course, with their polo shirts, visors, and khaki shorts. Finally, in the corner of the pool, were the serious drinking lesbians already guzzling their gin and tonics by 10:00 am. Then there were the pretty, forty-something, straight-looking, corporate lesbians from Bethesda, Maryland. At separate tables sat the military lesbians and the singles. Our people were nowhere in sight.

Marie and I had been together for thirteen years at this point. Like most finely tuned couples, we often read each other's minds. She looked at me and said, "Oh, Sweetie. I bet I know what you're thinking. You're afraid we won't fit in, right?"

I responded, "Well, there seem to be packs of lesbians. Everybody has a tribe. Maybe they have traveled together before."

Ever the optimist, Marie replied, "Well, we're both extroverts. Let's walk up to an interesting-looking couple and start a conversation. Things will pick up. Be hopeful!"

The next day, on my way back to our cabin to get my sunblock, I hurriedly turned the corner to enter the elevator when I ran into Billie Jean King. I was nervous and couldn't think of anything clever to say. The oddest crap tumbled out of my mouth.

In an excited, fourteen-year-old-sounding voice, I stammered, "Oh, hello, Ms. King! Wow, so nice to meet you! I'm Elizabeth. Thank you for being out for so long!"

I immediately wanted to die from embarrassment. How rude. I'd told Billie Jean King she was old as hell.

She snapped at me, "I didn't come out. I was outed by that ex of mine. It was nobody's business."

I turned tomato red.

"Oh, right. I'm so sorry."

We stepped onto the elevator, and Billie Jean said, "So, where are you from, anyway?"

"Washington, DC, but I was born and reared in a small town in Mississippi."

Billie Jean frowned and folded her arms.

"Oh well, that explains it!"

And she stepped off the elevator.

I was stunned.

The next day, Marie and I ran into the lesbian activist Edie Windsor on the beach. At eighty-four, she looked impressive in her black swimsuit with her fuchsia hat and matching fuchsia lipstick. She was so approachable and wanted to connect with us.

"Hey, girls. Isn't the ocean gorgeous?"

Marie and I give her hugs and thanked her for her hard work in suing the federal government and getting gay marriage passed at the federal level.

I exclaimed, "Ms. Windsor, thank you from the bottom of my heart for making sure that we get those 1,148 federal rights that married, straight people have! Marie and I married in San Francisco in 2008. I didn't think gay marriage would be legal for us for at least another ten years!"

Edie was beaming as she proclaimed, "Honey, you are so welcome. I never gave up on justice! After my dear partner of over forty years, Thea, died, I was furious that I had to pay the government over $350,000 in inheritance taxes! So, I found a young, smart, Jewish lesbian attorney, Roberta Kaplan (pro-bono, by the way). We sued the federal government. I thought it was a long shot, but we won! Now, I'm a lesbian celebrity! And I got all that money back. So now, I can go on all the Olivia cruises I want!"

When we got back to our ship, Marie went to hang out by the pool. I wanted to go back to the room and take a nap. I stepped back into the elevator, and noticed an older butch lesbian in a baseball cap.

She smiled, and with a deep southern accent said, "Good afternoon! What floor are you headed to, young lady?"

"Hello! The third floor, please. Where in the South are you from?"

"Near Vicksburg, Mississippi!"

I was thrilled to meet someone else from the Motherland!

"Oh, my God! I'm also from Mississippi. I don't know any other lesbians from our home state. I thought I was the only one... and Vicksburg! I went to a tiny Episcopal boarding school there, only for one year. You probably never heard of it–All Saints."

Her face lit up and she said, "All Saints! Yes, of course. Honey. I was the P.E. teacher and on the board there for over twenty-five years!"

And then it dawned on me. This was my P.E. teacher from high school, Ms. Dot. Some students had secretly called her "Dot, the Dyke," but I didn't know what that meant back in 1979.

"Oh my God! You're Ms. Dot, right?"

"I sure am, sugar. I'm Ms. Dot, Dorothy Ann Fitzgerald is my full name," she said with a captivating smile.

I remembered Ms. Dot as an encouraging P.E. teacher. I was not an athletic student, but she cheered me on and taught me how to water ski. Ms. Dot always made sure everyone was included and celebrated in the school games and even wrote a book about the importance of inclusion in education.

We got off the elevator and hugged in the hallway. I was that fifteen-year-old girl and fifty-year-old woman all at once.

"Oh, Ms. Dot, this is such synchronicity that we are on this Olivia cruise together. It's a small world. Are you here with a partner or a friend?"

"Well, I think it's a good thing that we are connecting now. I remember you as such a sweet and shy girl–not athletic, but smart. I'm here with my pack of girls from New Orleans. I saw my ex on the ship with her new girlfriend. And I'm so mad at her I could spit!"

The next morning was the last morning on the cruise. Marie and I had breakfast with Ms. Dot. She and Marie hit it off. They discovered they both loved golf and boats.

I stayed in touch with Ms. Dot for the next several months. One day, I got a text from her that said, "Hope y'all will come to my cabin for the reunion with my favorite students and fellow P.E. teachers and athletic directors the first weekend in June. We'll get out in my boat, play games, cook, eat, and tell stories!"

Wow, I was thrilled that Ms. Dot included us in this gathering of what I assumed would be all lesbians.

Marie and I made two trips down to visit her at her lovely log cabin on a lake in Louisiana, near Vicksburg. On the first trip, I flew down two days before Marie did, so I could have a leisurely visit with Ms. Dot. She told me her story of coming out in her late forties after she divorced her husband. I met her two lesbian friends, one of whom was a former student. We had dinner together, and I learned that her two friends were very closeted.

They whispered, "It's so good to meet someone like us. We can't talk about our lifestyle down here in Mississippi. We'd lose our jobs, and the Klan and the preachers would come after us!"

I was saddened and shocked. All three of these women, who were eleven to twenty years older than I, were terribly closeted. They'd never even been to a Pride Festival. There were no lesbian meet-up groups or potlucks in their conservative town. They had never experienced a larger lesbian culture. Coming out was not even a possibility for them.

One of Ms. Dot's friends, was a music teacher in the public school. Her partner had tragically died of cancer. She couldn't talk about it with her colleagues at school. She wasn't mentioned in the obituary. Her grief was invisible. I was grateful that I'd left Mississippi so many years before, and that I came out in Washington, DC in the 1990s when there was still a vibrant lesbian community.

The night before Marie arrived, Ms. Dot and I had a long conversation over dinner. With tears streaming down her cheeks, Ms. Dot confided,

"Lizbuth, it's been so hard for me. My brother doesn't let me see his kids or grandkids much. I know it's cause I'm gay. I know you've had a hard time with your family. Do we ever heal from this painful family rejection?"

I was touched by her vulnerability with me. Our roles had reversed. Now I got to be her teacher.

"Well, Ms. Dot, I'm still sad that I'm not connected to my siblings, and their kids, but that's no longer the focus of my life."

"What do you mean, Elizabeth?"

"Well, I've had a lot of therapy and support. I've grieved a lot. It's taken me a long time. I've learned to let go of my regrets about the past. I live more in the present now. Marie and my close friends are my family of choice, my family of heart. And now you are part of our tribe, right, Ms. Dot?"

"Absolutely, girl! You and Marie will always have a home here with me. We are definitely family now."

Six weeks later, Marie and I attended Ms. Dot's reunion with her students and colleagues, ten women from Los Angeles, most of whom were retired P.E. teachers and athletic directors. Many of them had met Ms. Dot when she taught continuing education classes in Southern California. Marie and I enjoyed meeting these women who were five to ten years older than us. We sat around the lake, went out on Ms. Dot's boat, and cooked pasta and seafood. We all stayed at Ms. Dot's beautiful log cabin. My personal jewel of the weekend was when I performed some stories from my one-woman play. I focused on telling my coming out story, including lesbian culture stories from the 1990s, stories about my first girlfriend, and meeting Marie. Later that night, the other women shared their coming out stories. It was a powerful evening of lesbian bonding in which we validated one another. I felt the incredible sense of belonging I'd been seeking.

CHAPTER 17

Sappho's Sex Den

B ack in DC, the oldest lesbian bar in the country, The Phase, had closed. Lesbian bookstores, dances, conferences, and retreats were disappearing. Assimilation and acceptance had happened, and there didn't seem to be much of a need for lesbian community. Potlucks were a thing of the past. Meet-up groups attracted young, single, queer-identified women. Marie and I are very lesbian-identified. While we understand the word "queer" has been reclaimed, we remembered it as a derogatory term growing up. I had heard from my friend, Lynne about how amazing the Michigan Women's Music Festival (Mich Fest) was. She called it "lesbian camp." I had wanted to go but never made it a priority because I didn't like to camp, and I hate August humidity. When the Michigan Women's Music Festival closed in 2015 after almost forty years in existence, I had to accept the hard reality I would never be able to attend. How I wish I had gone before it closed. I missed an iconic part of lesbian culture.

I miss hearing and seeing the word "lesbian." It seems like the word lesbian has been gradually fading from our language and from our consciousness. We've learned a great deal about trans, queer, and non-binary women, but I miss the old days of being a part of lesbian culture. It feels like there has been a cultural backlash. In the book, *The Disappearing L: Erasure of Lesbian Spaces and Culture* by women's studies professor, Bonnie J. Morris, she describes how, as lesbians, we are experiencing a "semantic phasing out, a three-fold dismissal of the word, and the female aspect of lesbian identity. The recent cultural history of lesbians is vanishing faster than a magician's handkerchief."

I believe part of the backlash against lesbians is generational. I've talked to younger women who love women, who identify as queer, and asked them why they do not identify with the word lesbian. They said they prefer the word queer because they experience their sexuality as more fluid. Many of them referred to the word "lesbian" as outdated and told me they associate it with angry, man-hating, feminists. I was shocked, and so are three generations of lesbian feminists who came out long ago and fought hard for our rights as women who love women. Perhaps part of the negative connotation of the word lesbian is about sexism, ageism, homophobia, and misogyny. I want to champion the word lesbian and lesbian spaces and culture.

Recently, I returned to sing in my LGBTQ+ chorus in Baltimore that I sang in for six years, from 2010 to 2016. I had been singing in a Unitarian church choir for a couple of years in DC where there were a number of gay men singing, but only a couple of lesbians. I missed being in the LGBTQ community. I especially wanted to connect with lesbians of my generation and with my lesbian elders.

It was time to immerse myself in the lesbian culture I was trying so hard to find. I'd heard of a women's music festival called SisterSpace in rural Maryland, a couple of hours from DC. I asked Marie to go with me, but she declined that invitation saying, "that's where the tattooed, crunchy lesbians go. Not my thing, but you go ahead, dear heart, and I'll stay here in our air-conditioned house with the dogs."

Somehow, in my twenty-three years of being out, I'd missed this unique lesbian cultural experience of attending a women's music festival. I'd heard and read about how empowering and fun these gatherings and festivals were, which provided safe spaces for lesbian workshops and entertainment.

I craved the company of lesbians my age (early fifties) and older. I've always admired the lesbian pioneers who came out in the 1960s and 70s. I had known a few older lesbians when Marie and I sang in the Lesbian and Gay Chorus of Washington, DC. I had been mesmerized hearing their coming out stories, some of which were heartbreaking, and some of which were hilarious.

SisterSpace held promise. Perhaps they'd be interested in me performing my one-woman play for the next year.

So, on a blazing September Friday afternoon, I left for Darlington, Maryland. I had made a reservation at a hotel, the Comfort Inn, in the nearest town, which was Aberdeen, about fourteen miles away. (I had learned that SisterSpace only had rough cabins and camping areas.) I emailed the director of the festival and received a special commuter day rate. It felt good that I was taking care of myself. It was the hottest day of the year, which was rare for the second weekend in September. I drove out to the camp and parked in the field. I saw an old barn and one other old building in the distance. My heart sank. I feared this place was going to be too much on the rustic side for someone like me. I yearned for sisterhood, not rustic cabins and sleeping bags. I don't do camping–ever. My idea of roughing it is staying at a Comfort Inn. I can commune with nature by looking at trees outside of a hotel room, protected from mosquitos, ticks, and other annoying insects.

I walked up to the registration table to find a stern-looking, older, butch woman.

She looked at me suspiciously and said, "Hey, I'm Billie. You staying in a cabin, or are you camping in your tent?"

I was quite horrified that she mentioned only those two options.

"Oh, no. I'm staying in town, in Aberdeen, at The Comfort Inn."

I smiled sweetly to mask my fear that she was going to tell me I had to stay at this run-down campground.

Billie frowned and said, "Well, women at SisterSpace don't usually leave the land. We stay here all weekend."

I was concerned as I envisioned uncomfortable images of sleeping on the ground, cold group showers, oppressive heat, and lots of maddening mosquitos.

I started to sweat like mad. My anxiety about being told I had to stay at this run-down camp only made things worse. It brought back memories of being forced to attend "pioneer camp" in Mississippi when I was ten, where we had to learn to pitch a tent and build a latrine. I was miserable as the only girly-girl non-camper. Once again, my old story of not belonging emerged.

I took a deep breath and looked Billie directly in the eye. "Well, you see. I'm a menopausal woman. And I must have air conditioning, a comfortable bed, and my own bathroom."

Billie frowned again. "Hmm. Did you get permission from JoAnn, our director, to do this? Did she give you a reduced day rate?"

"Yes, I spoke with JoAnne. She gave me the day rate."

"OK, then, but so you know, out of the two hundred women here, you are the only one staying at a hotel."

"Yes, I guessed that." I smiled and put my SisterSpace bracelet on with the yellow band that said "commuter." I was keenly aware that I would stand out in this crowd.

Out of nowhere, a young dyke with mermaid and snake tattoos all over her arms and nose rings hanging from her nostrils drove up to me on a golf cart.

"Hey, you need a ride to the dining hall where the check-in desk is located?"

"Oh, thanks, but I can manage the walk."

"Well, there are some steep hills to climb, and it's hot as hell today."

My ego was having a fit. Did this young thing think I was some frail, older woman? Did I look old and tired?

Hopefully not, but I was suffering in that humidity. It felt like the Egyptian desert, so I surrendered.

"Well, on second thought, sure, getting a ride with you would be great. Thanks, so much."

We rode up and down hills passing lots of older lesbians pitching tents and unloading their Subarus.

I got out of the golf cart and walked into the dining hall. I looked around and, to my amazement, almost every woman I saw was topless. Bare breasts everywhere of all sizes. Some had nipple piercings. And some women were totally naked. As a Southern woman who values modesty, I was shocked and uncomfortable.

I looked pretty mainstream in my khaki shorts, rainbow t-shirt that said "Relentlessly Gay," silver sandals, and carrying my lavender purse. I felt ridiculous, like I was in the seventh grade at the school dance wearing the wrong outfit. Hell, here at SisterSpace, I was the only one in an outfit!

I texted Marie. "Holy Shit! Naked, hairy, tattooed lesbians everywhere. Not one other lipstick lesbian. Maybe this is not my crowd! Should I come home?"

Marie responded, "LOL! No, stay for the story, sweetie!"

I sat down to fan myself and drink some water. An older woman wearing long dreadlocks sat beside me.

"You're a virgin, right?" she asked.

"Pardon me?"

"You're a SisterSpace virgin. This is your first time here, right?"

"Yes, how can you tell?"

"Well, you have all your clothes on for one thing. And you look nervous. My advice is to lose the purse and turn off your phone. We're not allowed to take pictures. A lot of women want their privacy here. This is a safe space for everyone."

"Ok, thanks for the tips." I thought about what an uncomfortably long weekend this was going to be.

I don't mean to sound judgmental, but I was shocked by this edgy lesbian culture. Where were the lesbians who looked like me? Although I thought of myself as an open-minded, liberal-leaning, lesbian, I felt traditional around these lesbians.

I don't do public nudity. Never have and never will. I'm not edgy or crunchy. I shave my legs and underarms every day from May through October. I wear make-up and blow-dry and curl my hair. Sometimes I wear silver or lavender nail polish. I identify as femme lesbian and as a feminist. I've been criticized by other lesbians for "looking like a straight, suburban woman." I realize that I do have privilege over some lesbians who look more butch. I'm comfortable with who I am and how I look. I also embrace the values of feminism. I love hearing older feminist lesbians' stories from back in the day. I looked forward to hearing my elders' stories.

That afternoon, I ran into a woman, Linda, who used to date a friend of mine. She invited me into the house where she and her new girlfriend were staying. I didn't realize folks could stay there. It was an old Victorian house from the Civil War era that used to have an underground escape route for slaves. There was a rainbow flag flying on the front porch and sex toys displayed on a table for sale. Linda told me they were having a happy hour.

I walked into the house called "Sappho's Sex Den", and went into a room to the right, which was called "Mighty Aphrodite." There were red candles and large dildos, boxes of Kleenex, towels and two beds in there. It was for people who wanted to engage in consensual erotic play. There was a sign-up list on the door, so women could schedule their "playtime." The other room had black leather contraptions that I'd never seen for the folks into bondage/SM play. This was not my scene. I quickly left this room.

An elderly, topless woman with purple leggings approached me in the hallway.

"Hi, I'm Helga. A little bondage, dear? Are you here to play?"

I was shocked. Helga appeared to be in her mid-eighties. She looked like a friendly, wholesome grandma.

"No, ma'am. I'm a married, monogamous, vanilla lesbian."

Helga looked disappointed and confused. Then she started to tell me about her experiences as a sex slave in Europe and how she was turned on by bondage and being whipped.

This was too much for me. So, I tried to distract her from her sex stories.

"Helga, tell me your coming out story."

"Oh, I'm not a lesbian, dear. I'm just adventurous."

"Well, how did you find out about SisterSpace?" I asked.

"Oh, some nice ladies at my Unitarian Church told me about this place seven years ago. I've been coming every year. I'm the honorary crone around here. Everyone loves to touch me during our community playtime. And my great-grandchildren think I'm cool!"

We went out onto the front porch to have some iced tea. Then a younger woman came running up to us with her large bouncing breasts leading the way. She said, "Everyone is invited to the erotic games on the lawn."

I looked out in the front yard and saw all ages of women, in various states of naked with balloons attached to their rear ends. It was apparently a relay race to get people to do pelvic thrusts and pop the balloons.

Then, a tall, butch, bronze woman came over to me as I was applying my magenta lipstick to distract myself from the action.

"You got some lipstick that you can wear to kiss my wife's breasts with, so she'll have some lip prints on her tits?"

At first, I had no words. Sometimes my life seems like an entertaining movie unfolding. I said nothing and pretended I didn't hear her.

She persisted. "Hey, femmie girl, do you want to kiss my wife's breasts or not?"

Her beautiful, curvy wife appeared in a black leather bustier, with the most ample cleavage I'd ever seen.

"No, thank you," I said.

Helga chimed in and said, "I will! I will!"

Helga wanted to borrow my lipstick. I gave it to her, and Helga planted a lovely imprint of her lips in the woman's cleavage.

In that moment, I stopped judging them. I realized these women were much more comfortable with their sexuality than I was. How freeing that must be.

Later that evening, a bunch of us were in the pool. I was one of the few in a swimsuit. I was telling one of my coming out stories from my one-woman play. The naked, butch lesbians swam over to me to listen. Everyone nodded and laughed at my "Coming Out at Mama's Funeral" story. Others began to share their stories. Magically, we were connected through sharing our stories.

One of the butch women said, "Hey, Miss Lesbian Belle, you should lose your suit!"

I smiled and winked. "Maybe next year!"

CHAPTER 18

Reframing Southern Comfort

"The truth is that telling heals. Not just once, but as a way of being that filters the heart of its debris. And once the telling begins, experience becomes a strange storyteller. Often, it shows us how to lose and how to heal. Often, it shows us how to face what seems unacceptable. Events stranger than dreams come into being and we are left to find the medicine."

– *Mark Nepo*

As I was finishing writing this book, my siblings, cousins, and I sold our beloved summer home, Southern Comfort, which we had inherited together. Joint ownership among six family members who live in different parts of the country had been stressful. It was hard for us to make decisions together about renovations needed in this house built in 1885. It was getting very expensive. Still, I loved my childhood and teenage summers on that mountain–especially in that big, old house. Memories of cool summer breezes on July afternoons listening to Mama and her sisters tell stories about their

Mississippi Delta childhood filled my heart and mind. I could still see their poofy silver hairdo helmets, and their tangerine, crimson red, and fuchsia-colored lips. I remembered Aunt Frannie's pretty, bejeweled sandals, which she wore in her younger days, and the way she would pat me and say, "I love you so much, you precious girl." And how could I forget the scent and sound of Aunt Liber lighting her Winston cigarette, which she elegantly pulled from her red and gold leather cigarette case. She'd have a scotch on the side table, as she launched into another tall Delta tale. Other memories surfaced—like going to the pool and movies with my childhood pals. I could smell the chlorine at the pool, and the buttered popcorn at the snack shop at the movie theatre. And, of course, there were those fourth of July picnics with Mama and Daddy, my aunts, uncles, and cousins on the Mall, the public park between the dining hall and the chapel.

I loved Southern Comfort and the village of Monteagle Assembly as a child, teen, and young woman. But the reality was that for eight years after I'd come out in my thirties, Mama wouldn't let me visit her and her sisters and Southern Comfort. I still remember the sting of Mama telling me that I couldn't come. She couldn't give me a specific reason. She said that it wasn't a good idea. After Mama and her sisters died, and my siblings and cousins and I inherited the house, I could finally bring Marie. We went for several Fourth of July long weekends where there were many cousins and their friends, most of whom we didn't know very well. And as far as I knew, Marie and I were the only out lesbian couple on the entire mountain—hell, probably within a hundred miles. This Christian, gated community tends to be traditional, white, and privileged. Monteagle Assembly people are good people – very conservative, except for a few artists and feminists.

I decided I wanted to have a final house party at Southern Comfort that October, a few months before we put the house on the market and when the fall colors would be vibrant. Some of my favorite teachers from my boarding school days at St. Andrew's–Sewanee lived nearby. They weren't getting any younger. Marie and I had friends in Asheville, a four-hour drive away who had never seen the house. I thought it would be fun and meaningful to perform my one-woman play, *A Lesbian Belle Tells…* at Southern Comfort for them.

A few days before the house party and performance, I drove to Tennessee to do a thorough housecleaning of Southern Comfort, and to do a goodbye ritual before Marie and our friends arrived. I also wanted to have one-on-one visits with my beloved teacher, Mr. Ham, from my boarding school, and with my childhood friend, Christi Teasley.

When I arrived at Southern Comfort, much to my horror, I saw wasps everywhere – darting above my head, and into toilets and beds. The entire house was infested with these wild wasps. I had to call an exterminator.

Over the next three days, I encountered unexpected moments of synchronicity and grace. I was staying at a hotel down the road while the wasps were dying. The first night, my key card didn't work to get into the room. It was past midnight, and I was exhausted from the eleven-hour drive from Maryland. I went to the front desk to get another key card. The young man on the night shift was a giant–over seven feet tall. When I explained about needing another key card, he calmly said, "No problem. I'll get you another one. By the way, I like your Goddess necklace, ma'am." I couldn't believe that a guy in Tennessee recognized the Goddess!

I exclaimed, "How do people in Tennessee know about the Goddess? Are you Pagan?"

In a monotone voice, he said, "Yes, ma'am, and gay, too! There are three of us here on the mountain. We have a queer magic circle every month. By the way, my Spirit name is Angel."

What a moment. This was exactly what I needed, meeting a gay, kindred soul. I mentioned my wife, and he smiled. Each morning, Angel greeted me, and we shared brief conversations about our favorite Tarot decks. He reminded me to do a purification releasing ritual before I left Southern Comfort using sage and sweetgrass so I would not carry any negative energy with me as I traveled home. It was grounding to talk to Angel, especially since I was only getting two or three hours of sleep a night. I woke up every morning at 3:00 am with relentless sobbing. In Chinese medicine, this is known as a time when the grief arises. Southern Comfort held the loving magical memories from my childhood. I was also grieving those eight summers when I couldn't visit. It was so hard to let go of that incredible house.

On the third morning at the hotel, Angel asked me for a ride home and offered to show me where the "hippy store" was to buy some sweetgrass. (He said he needed some lavender for a handfasting ritual he was planning with his new boyfriend he'd met on Grindr.) I agreed to drive him home. At the hippy store, I chatted with the salesclerk, Jean, a gray-haired woman in her late fifties. She asked me if I had grown up on the mountain. When I told her I'd spent childhood summers there but that I was originally from Mississippi, Jean piped up animatedly and said,

"Good Lord, so am I!"

Feeling an instant connection, I said, "Oh, really, where? I'm from Okolona, near Tupelo."

Jean smiled and said, "Well, I'm from Natchez."

At this point, I fell into my Mississippi, nice girl syndrome and exclaimed,

"Oh, Natchez! I loved going to y'all's pilgrimage and seeing those beautiful antebellum homes!"

I thought I was giving her a hometown compliment.

To my surprise, Jean frowned and yelled, "I hated those damn Barbie doll girls in the hoop skirts who displayed themselves on those porches during that awful pilgrimage weekend. I was a tomboy, and those girls looked down their noses at me."

You know what? I thought Jean was coming out to me. She still had that tomboy look, and I was sure she was a middle-aged, butch lesbian. So, I said, "I know what you mean, Jean. When I came out, there was such drama in my family."

Jean said, "Oh, you had one of those awful debutante coming out balls?"

I replied, "Hell no, Jean. I'm not talking about coming out as a debutante. I'm talking about coming out as a lesbian!"

We all laughed heartily, the way Southerners do when we connect over the eccentricities of our culture.

I had plans to spend most of the next day with one of my favorite boarding-school teachers, Mr. Eugene Ham. Mr. Ham made American history and American literature come alive in his classroom back in 1980. I had invited him to have lunch and then accompany me back to Southern Comfort to do a goodbye ritual. His mind was still sharp now at seventy-three. One minute he would be quoting Flannery O'Connor, and the next minute he would mention an article he'd read in *The New Yorker Magazine*. Mr. Ham and I had a strong Mississippi connection. He grew up in the Delta, in Greenville, which was close to my mother's hometown, Indianola.

Mr. Ham represented the best of the eccentric, liberal South. He was (and is) articulate, intellectual, progressive, and every bit a Southern gentleman. I adore his polite, kind, and refined Delta accent that is rare to find these days.

I had reconnected with Mr. Ham about ten years ago when Marie and I were staying at Southern Comfort. I had casually come out to him on the phone, mentioning that my partner's name was

Marie. His response was, "I'm looking forward to meeting Marie and getting to know her. Would you two ladies like to dine with me for lunch at my house?" We were delighted to be welcomed into his home, in Fayetteville, Tennessee, where he served us chicken salad sandwiches, stuffed eggs, juicy red tomato slices, and of course, sweet tea.

That crisp October afternoon back in 2009, Mr. Ham drove us out to his grandparents' farmhouse that had been in his family since the 1840s. I was reminded of his passion for telling a tale as he exclaimed,

"By jingo, ladies, step into the front room and see the very bed which that rascal Sherman slept in during a battle in the War of Northern Aggression, when they invaded this part of Tennessee. Of course, we've changed the mattress and the sheets since then!"

During this visit with Mr. Ham, I noticed that he looked a bit older and thinner. I was comforted to see him wearing the same kind of traditional men's clothes I remembered him wearing in 1980, when he was my American history teacher. He wore his blue, oxford cloth shirt, khaki pants, and his round, tortoise-shell glasses, and rugged hiking shoes. He still had that sensible Southern academic look.

Mr. Ham only recently got a cell phone—a flip phone, not an iPhone. He doesn't do email or Facebook, which I find refreshing. He is truly present in the moment and still values leisurely porch visits. Mr. Ham still believes that Southern porch time is sacred visiting time. He's certainly not in a hurry.

After lunch at Papa Ron's Italian restaurant, we went back to Southern Comfort. I read Mr. Ham the chapter about the porch stories, and my grandparents' love letters, which delighted him. He offered me insightful and supportive feedback about my writing.

I asked Mr. Ham to walk with me through every room in the house with the sage to thank the house and release it. He lit up and said, "Oh, yes! Sage, from the Native American tradition. A powerful purification ritual." I said a prayer of thanksgiving to my ancestors–Mama, Aunt Liber, and Aunt Frannie. I released the old energy from the past.

As we slowly moved through each room, Mr. Ham commented on the details he loved–the glass doorknobs, the numbers on the bedroom doors from when it was a boarding house, the Victorian bedroom furniture, and the double wrap-around porch that was a classic Queen Anne architectural style. This helped me savor each room. Then we walked around the house, and I placed three red crystal hearts in various hidden places to honor the three sisters.

On an unromantic note, the next day, I had to call a plumber, Mr. King, to unclog a stopped-up toilet.

I was stressed and in a hurry to meet my friend, Christi, for a walk at 3:00 pm. When Mr. King arrived, I immediately noticed his kind, dark brown eyes. I introduced myself to him. With a twinkle in his eyes, he said, "I sure do miss the three sisters, Miss Liber, Miss Nita, and can't remember the third one's name–the Ohio sister."

"My Aunt Frannie! My God, Mr. King. You knew my mother and my aunts?"

"Sure did, 'cause I been unstopping these toilets for over forty years." We shared a good chuckle together. I realized that I was in the house as a little girl when he worked on the plumbing.

I immediately teared up, and so did Mr. King. He had known and served my family for all those years. I loved this personal connection that often happens in small Southern towns.

"Can I tell you a tale?" Mr. King asked.

"Oh, please, Mr. King. Do tell."

"Well, one day, your mama called me to get some critters out of the attic. I got up there and saw them bats. I told her that I couldn't do that job 'cause I have a fear of bats."

"Wow, Mr. King, so do I. I remember waking up in the middle of the night with bats flying out of the attic. It was creepy."

"Yeah, they hired somebody else. Your mama told me not to tell your daddy about the bats. She said if he knew about them, he'd never come back to visit. So I didn't tell him. I've been telling that story for over forty years, but I never mention your mother's name."

We laughed and marveled about those bats. (By the way, the spiritual symbolism of the bat is death and rebirth, which was a reminder of the larger meaning of letting go of Southern Comfort.)

As Mr. King was about to leave, he paused and said, "Have you got time for one more tale?"

"Absolutely, Mr. King." I was savoring every moment with him.

"Well, your brother called me at midnight one Friday night, a few years ago. I wondered what on earth he wanted. I answered the phone and heard all this loud music. Turned out, he was at a party, and he had butt-dialed me."

We both cracked up again. I gave Mr. King a tip and thanked him. "You have no idea how much you brightened my day with your stories about my family."

"I'm glad to share, ma'am. This house is a grand one. It's gone down, though, and needs a lot of work. Can I ask why y'all are selling it?"

I was used to this question by now and had my answer ready.

"With joint ownership among six family members and the expenses of the upkeep, it became apparent to us that it was time to let it go."

"I understand. My siblings and I sold our parents' house a few years ago. It's hard to let a house go, but you'll always have the memories."

Mr. King was a much-needed story guide for me that day. His stories reminded me about the power of slowing down and being present. All it takes is one simple story shared to connect us with one another.

My friend, Christi, came over, and we took a long walk through Monteagle Assembly, out to the cemetery, and to the Point, a place at the edge of the mountain with an overlook onto the valley below. We also walked by the swimming pool, where Christi reminded me of our water ballet classes where we jumped to the tune of the Pink Panther one year. We must have been nine and ten years old. Christi even remembered the specific strokes we did. She did an air version of our routine which we performed at the Hawaiian Luau back in the 1970s. We laughed as we recalled the pink tails we had attached to our swimsuits.

When we got back to Southern Comfort, Christi took final pictures of me in front of the house. I thanked her for spending so much time with me. Christi is a talented fiber artist and keeps a tight schedule. She had also brought a dinner of pizza and prosecco for our last meal at Southern Comfort the night before and had stayed for three hours.

I reflected on our time together and said, "Christi, this was so special that we got in two visits this weekend. This is more time than we've spent together in years."

Christi smiled and said, "Elizabeth, you said something last night that impacted me in a positive way. You said you are setting an intention in your life to slow down and be present with people, instead of rushing on to the next thing. When I got home last night, my husband, Carlton, commented on how late I was out and reminded me that I said I was going to be home by 8:00 pm to finish my next art project. And I told him what you said."

"Thanks, Christi. Porch visits beat being productive any day!"

The house party was a blast. Our dear Asheville friend, Martha, had prepared the food, which we so appreciated. I loved seeing my teachers and classmates connect with one another. I was delighted that

they came. Susan Core, my Southern literature teacher, still looked
vibrant and elegant at eighty. Sandford McGee, my biology teacher,
was an active sixty-seven year old. And Mr. Ham was quoting *The
Glass Menagerie*, "Memory is seated predominantly in the heart." I
was happy to hear the joyful sound of laughter on the porch again.
I loved performing my play for everyone in the living room. Marie
was helpful with the music and the photographs on the projector. I
can't tell you how healing it was to tell my stories in the very house
that gifted me with the love for storytelling throughout my childhood.
Since I was forbidden from visiting Southern Comfort after I came
out, it was especially poignant and healing to host this party and tell
my most moving and painful family stories to my boarding school
teachers and classmates and my present-day friends from Asheville.
My past and present were integrated. I had come full circle.

My teachers were noticeably touched. Tears, gasps, and laughter
filled the room as I told my stories. None of them had known the
details or the complications of my coming out story. There was an
awkward moment after I performed. I asked if people wanted to
share some of their own stories or offer me feedback. I felt raw and
vulnerable. Then one of my classmates, Natalie, held her hand up. I
got nervous because she was not smiling. I couldn't read her face. We
were not close during our school days in the 1980s. She was popular
and hilarious as part of the cool, wild crowd. I was strait-laced, shy,
and quiet. Our connection had been the chorus, but I never thought
Natalie liked me. I felt my seventeen year old insecurity rise up as
Natalie began to speak with a tone of authority, "I admit I didn't
know what you were gonna talk about performing for an hour. I
honestly didn't think this would be very good, but I must say your
performance was incredible. I laughed, and I cried. I'm not a lesbian,
but I connected with the humanity of your stories."

I was surprised and pleased to hear that I had touched Natalie. I felt my appreciation deepen for everyone there. The pain of family rejection faded. I realized the value of being in the present moment and feeling a sense of belonging within myself, which then helps me feel more connected to people I love.

Throughout the weekend, my friend, Martha, mentioned that she felt the presence of the three sisters. I was distracted cleaning and being a hostess the first couple of times she mentioned their energy. Suddenly, she got my attention when she said, "Elizabeth, who called you 'Baby Girl'? I keep hearing an older woman calling out 'Baby Girl' over and over."

Well, this stopped me dead in my tracks. No pun intended. In my childhood and adolescence, Aunt Liber frequently would say to me, "Baby girl, let's go sit out on the porch. I'll tell you stories about growing up that your Mama doesn't even know."

The last morning, I asked Martha to sit down and see if she had more messages from the spirit world she wanted to share. She agreed, and I recorded her on my phone. Martha apparently had psychic gifts since childhood. The messages she gave me felt spot on. I will tell you in advance that Martha knew little about my mother and aunts. She had never met them. For about forty-five minutes, Martha gave me messages from the three sisters. She told me they were thrilled that I performed my show in Southern Comfort and that they love me so much. They were glad I was carrying their legacy of storytelling and bringing it out into the world. Martha also shared that Aunt Liber said it was hard for their generation as women in a patriarchal Southern culture. She said the men had all the power, and her frustration in feeling powerless drove her to drink too much. Then Martha shared messages from my mother.

"Well, your mother's very proud of you and loves you so much. She feels guilty and is asking for your forgiveness. She said that while she was alive, she wasn't evolved enough to accept your sexuality. She says she has such remorse now. She regrets that she caused you so much pain."

I was speechless and in tears. Finally, I got an apology from Mama. I wish she could have asked for my forgiveness while she was alive, but I was grateful to hear from her in spirit. I can honestly say I had already forgiven her years ago.

I realized that my relationship with this house was not ending. I carry within me the legacy of my ancestor's stories and the gifts of Southern Comfort. I have learned how to reframe my Southern experience. I no longer needed to own this house. I no longer needed to cling to the past. That goodbye visit in Tennessee helped me grieve well, appreciate the past, and savor the present moment. My stories of loss, healing, and discovery now live on in this book and my one-woman play. These stories will always reside in my heart.

I had integrated the lessons of letting go, forgiving, and moving on to the next chapter of my life. I accepted that loss is a natural part of the cycle of death and rebirth. I could now embrace a sense of belonging within myself, my family-of-choice, and my extended community. Most importantly, I had given myself the gift of accepting and loving my story with compassion and gratitude for every single chapter.

POSTSCRIPT

"Our job is not to deny the story, but to defy the ending—to rise strong, recognize our own story, and rumble with the truth until we get to a place where we think YES. This is what happened. This is my truth. And I choose how the story ends."
- Brené Brown, Ph.D.

As LGBTQ+ people, I believe one of the greatest gifts we can give to one another is our authentic stories told from our hearts. Collectively, we have so many heartbreaking and triumphant stories of coming out, feeling different, dating, breaking up, celebrating in gay bars, feeling abandoned, partying at Pride festivals, falling in love, forgiving, and finding acceptance and belonging.

Many of us long for more in-person connection with our friends, families, and communities. We have too much connection through technological screens that do not provide the intimate heart connections we all need as human beings. We can go days without even hearing a human voice, with all our texting, emailing, and messaging. It's easy to become lonely and isolated.

I believe that the antidote for this disconnection and suffering is storytelling. When we share our stories with one another, magic happens. We are seen and heard. We validate one another and offer consolation and comfort to one another. We realize we are no longer alone. We find hope again. Storytelling in community, even with one other person, can shift us into meaningful connection when moments earlier we felt alone.

It is sometimes easy to cling to painful stories from the past. The good news is that we have a choice on what kind of perspective we have of our personal narratives. We can release our family stories that no longer serve us. We can embrace a more empowered and positive view of our stories. It is up to us as LGBTQ+ people to rise up from our inner darkness, turn the key to our own closets of oppression and internalized homophobia, and let ourselves out. As writer Alice Walker wisely wrote, "We are the ones we've been waiting for because we are able to see what is happening with a much greater awareness than our parents, or grandparents, or ancestors could see."

We can choose to live with gratitude for all the stories that make us who we are. From our soul's perspective, we can see that stories happen for us and not to us. Our stories keep unfolding for our healing, growth, and transformation.

No matter how painful your stories might be, I hope you can find the lessons in them and discover your own pot of gold at the end of your rainbow. As Brené Brown, world-renown social work research professor, writes, we can "rise strong" together and choose how our story ends. I believe there are always gifts that come to us during and after our darkest days. We need to keep our hearts open to them.

Remember that you are the author and heroine or hero of your own life story. No one else on the planet can tell or write your unique stories. You are the only one who can decide when it is time to let go of a painful story, savor a delightful story, and proclaim when it is time to live a new story.

Here is the bottom line–we cannot change the past, but we can choose to live in the present moment with more peace. We can discover a future ripe with possibility, love, and connection. Life is what we make it. We have everything we need inside us to create meaningful lives and to awaken to our own liberating stories.

Brené Brown defines vulnerability as "uncertainty, risk, and emotional exposure." The magic of storytelling brings us back into belonging with one another through our vulnerability. And in these chaotic times in which we live with too much work, technology, political disasters, and disconnection, we need authentic in-person connection, now more than ever.

Thank you for reading my memoir and journeying with me through these stories. May you have the courage and commitment to remember your personal stories, and feel the full range of your emotions with compassion for yourself and your loved ones. May you reach a place in your heart where loss and love coexist. Above all, may you accept and celebrate your whole life story with pride–every single chapter.

QUESTIONS FOR AN LGBTQ+ STORYTELLING DISCUSSION GROUP

1. When did you first realize you were attracted to a lesbian, gay, bisexual, queer, or transgender person? How did you feel?
2. Tell one of your favorite stories about your first kiss or date.
3. What was your experience of your first LGBTQ+ event, lesbian potluck, dance, gay bar, or your first women's music festival?
4. Do you identify as lesbian, bisexual, queer, transgender, or some other term? Discuss why sexual orientation and/or gender identity matters to you (or why it doesn't.)
5. Does your family-of-origin accept you? If you are partnered or married, how does your family treat the two of you as a couple?
6. How out are you? What gives you the courage to live out with pride?
7. Who are your LGBTQ+ role models beyond celebrity ones? How can you develop or deepen these relationships?

8. What losses have you experienced? (Include people who have died, relationships that have ended, your aging process, and life transitions.) How have you changed and grown through your grieving process?

9. What does forgiveness mean to you?

   a. For what do you need to forgive yourself?

   b. Who do you want to forgive and release?

   c. From whom might you need to ask forgiveness?

10. What story from your past no longer serves you? What can your new story be that fills you with hope, possibility, and a positive outlook?

11. Where do you find meaningful community connections?

   a. Has community faded from your life? If so, why and how?

   b. How can you develop or revive a sense of belonging in your life?

12. Who are your closest friends?

   a. How often do you see them?

   b. What prevents you from getting together more often?

   c. How can you deepen your friendships?

13. For singles – What are ten qualities you want in your ideal partnership with another person? (Be specific.)

14. For couples – How can you deepen your relationship and be a better partner or spouse? How can you have more fun together as a couple?

15. How can you bring more joy, play, and laughter into your life?

ACKNOWLEDGMENTS

Writing this book has been a long journey with unexpected twists and turns. It has taken a village of dedicated people who have supported and inspired me along the way. To my beloved spouse, Marie, I am deeply grateful for your abiding love, grounding presence, and your attention to the practical details. You are my soulmate, best friend, and anchor. Thank you for hearing and experiencing so many of my and our stories through our nineteen years together. Your encouragement and assistance with technology provided a crucial foundation for my writing. I love you to the moon and back!

To my friend and graphic designer, Heidi Fosnaught, thank you for creating a beautiful cover design, formatting the photographs, and keeping me focused during stressful days.

I was fortunate to receive helpful feedback on the first rough draft of this memoir from my beta readers. Lynne Barstow, your editing gave me excellent, honest feedback on what worked well and what needed polishing. Thank you for your friendship and generosity of time and energy.

Thank you to my publisher, Crystal Heart Imprints, Ruth Souther, for your guidance, mentorship, and laughter through the writing and publishing process. You are a Priestess extraordinaire!

To writing retreat leaders, Christine Kloser and Peggy Tabor Millin, thank you for holding sacred space at your retreats, which gave me uninterrupted time to write.

Thank you, Carrie Jareed, for your encouragement and excellent attention to details.

I appreciated and benefitted from writing classes on memoir writing, publishing, and marketing from The Writer's Center in Bethesda, Maryland.

To Mama, Marguerite Cooper McCain, and her two sisters, Elizabeth Cooper Prichard, and Frances Cooper Stonebraker, and my cousins at our summer home called "Southern Comfort," thank you for the many hours of leisurely stories told on the porch, which inspired me to become a storyteller. I treasure those memories.

I am especially grateful for the wisdom of my soul and the spirit world. Thank you to my Celtic ancestors, and my creative Higher Power for guiding me through the writing and birthing of this book.

ABOUT THE AUTHOR

Story is the heart and soul of Elizabeth McCain's work. She brings almost thirty years of professional experience as a psychotherapist, spiritual counselor, and workshop leader. Elizabeth is also a transformational storyteller, life story coach, an ordained interfaith minister, and an energy therapist.

Elizabeth has written and performed an award-winning one-woman play, *A Lesbian Belle Tells...*, for Pride festivals, queer theater festivals, Fringe theater festivals, government agencies, community centers, house concerts, and spiritual retreats. She has taught workshops on grief and loss, forgiveness, authentic spirituality,

slowing down for soul care, the power of LGBTQ+ stories, reviving lesbian community, and deepening women's friendships.

Whether counseling, coaching, ministering, or performing, Elizabeth's mission is to support and inspire LGBTQ+ people in sharing and reframing their personal stories of coming out/living out, loss, love, and transition for personal growth, transformation, and community building. She believes that sharing our stories from the wisdom of the soul with one another in community heals hearts and changes the world.

Elizabeth holds a B.A. in English from Randolph-Macon Woman's College, an M.A. in Counseling and Human Development from The George Washington University, and has received training in Imago relationship therapy, positive psychology, soul directed leadership, clinical and process acupressure, shamanic breathwork, and ancestral healing. She is an ordained interfaith minister and completed an interfaith studies program from The Chaplaincy Institute in Berkeley, California.

She has received storytelling, theater, and comedy coaching from storytellers and actors in Washington, DC, Santa Fe, and Asheville, North Carolina.

Elizabeth also supports terminally ill people in reviewing and sharing their life stories to create a meaningful legacy. Her heart has been cracked open by her own sorrow and joy in her personal journey through loss and grief.

Elizabeth resides in the Maryland suburbs near Washington, DC, with her spouse, Marie, and their two adorable dogs, Lucy and Teddy. She enjoys singing with The New Wave LGBTQ+ Singers of Baltimore, travel, theater, meditation, and gathering with friends for sharing all kinds of stories.

To learn how to work personally with Elizabeth or book her for a storytelling performance or speaking engagement, visit her at www.elizabethmccain.com.

Will you post a review on Amazon?

If you like what you read in

A Lesbian Belle Tells, I'd greatly appreciate if

you'd post a review on Amazon.

This will help me reach more people.

Thank you! Go here to post your review:

www.alesbianbelletells.com/amazon-reviews/

Made in the USA
Middletown, DE
27 December 2020